THE WAYS OF THE DESERT

The Ways of the Desert

by GENERAL E. DAUMAS

NINTH EDITION

REVISED AND AUGMENTED

WITH COMMENTARIES BY

The Emir Abd-el-Kader

Translated from the French by
SHEILA M. OHLENDORF

With a Foreword by
ROBERT A. FERNEA

UNIVERSITY OF TEXAS PRESS, AUSTIN & LONDON

International Standard Book Number 0-292-70087-3
Library of Congress Catalog Card Number 73-140171
Copyright © 1971 by Sheila M. Ohlendorf
All rights reserved
Type set by G&S Typesetters, Austin
Printed by Capital Printing Company, Austin
Bound by Universal Bookbindery, Inc., San Antonio

FOR OHLIE

WHO

GAVE ME

PEPPY RAB

(IAHA A 25619)

FOREWORD

North African studies, until recently the almost exclusive province of French scholarship, has in the last decade become a subject of increasing interest on this side of the Atlantic. *The Ways of the Desert,* previously available only in French, responds to this interest by offering the reader a fascinating introduction to the life of the North African Arab nomad. Its companion volume, *Horses of the Sahara,* provided a detailed description and history of the great breeds of Arab horses; *The Ways of the Desert* not only shows us how these horses are used, but adds detailed information about related activities in the Sahara desert.

The appeal of this volume goes well beyond its attractions for those of us with a special interest in the lore of desert hunt and chase. General Daumas and his major collaborator-informant, the Emir Abd-el-Kader, together provide sensitive insights into the total culture of the North African desert people of the nineteenth century. Both spiritual and material aspects of desert life are encompassed in this work, which ranges from translations of Arab poetry to descriptions of the uses of the fat and remains of the ostrich! The patterns of conviction and conduct described form an important part of the rich cultural heritage of the modern Maghreb nations.

General Daumas had the tastes and style of an ethnologist if not the formal training, for his descriptions are clearly built upon interviews with native informants who were experts in their particular line of activity. Thus the way of life described in this book is often presented from what comes very close to being an inside point of view. Occasionally the good General feels obliged to indicate his disapproval of certain practices or beliefs or to criticize his Arab friends, but in large part his underlying sympathy for the Arab people of the North African desert overcomes his conventionalized ethnocentrisms and permits his informants to speak clearly through his pen.

A great part of the book is devoted to the descriptions of the various animals that are both hunted and used for hunting. The reader, however, will find also a great deal of information about tribal customs and the problems of the domestic tent. So also will he discover something of the Arab nomads' religious feeling, thus gaining a view of Islam quite different from that reflected in the formal statements of those scholars who find the principle more interesting than the practice.

This is a charming book, charming in the most positive sense of the word. The style, happily conveyed in Mrs. Ohlendorf's excellent translation, serves well the educated French General, the Arab aristocrat, and the Arab nomads, whose views are all well portrayed. General Daumas did not attempt social analysis: He was not interested in resolving academic problems. He has, however, provided us with an ethnography which compares favorably with the best of the travel literature of the nineteenth century, and which greatly enhances our understanding of North African life today. We are in Mrs. Ohlendorf's debt for making it available to a new readership.

ROBERT A. FERNEA

Director, Center for Middle Eastern Studies
The University of Texas

CONTENTS

ILLUSTRATIONS

(Following page 114)

TRANSLATOR'S INTRODUCTION

The present book is a logical complement to *The Horses of the Sahara*, of which it is the second half. The work originally appeared in French under the title *The Horses of the Sahara and the Ways of the Desert*. In the first half of his work, which dealt in full with the Saharian Barb, the author discussed only incidentally the Arab tribes of the Sahara, the nomads who breed the Barbs. In this book, the second half, the author treats more specifically of the desert people—their customs, traditions, dress, and so forth. Both works, together or separately, provide an invaluable insight into life in Algeria during the French regime and should prove useful to historians, ethnologists, and to the general reader as well.

Neither of these works is very well known to the English-reading public because of a grave disservice done them in 1863 when they were translated into English for the first and, until 1968, the last time. The 1863 translation was so heavily bowdlerized as to make it useless, thus causing Lady Wentworth, the late eminent authority on the Arabian horse, to summarily dismiss it as a collection of Algerian fairy tales. Had she troubled to read the original French she would have found a great deal concerning the horses she loved so much, as pertinent today as it was in 1850.

Be that as it may, the reader, interested in the Arab-Barb controversy or not, will find much that is absorbing in both of these works, which, because they were well written to begin with, have made this translator's task more engrossing and much easier.

THE WAYS OF THE DESERT

1

THE NOMADS OF THE SAHARA

> Be gone, strangers, be gone!
> Leave the flowers of our meadows
> For the bees of our land.
> Be gone, strangers, be gone!
>
> (Chant of the Oulad Yacoub)

Upon describing with a scrupulous exactitude the assiduity with which
the Arabs attend their horses, the qualities which they seek to develop
in them, I have only indicated the goal they set themselves. That which
the man of the desert desires, that which he most often obtains—
thanks to his vigilant solicitude—is a swift, strong horse; toughened,
as they say. The true war-horse. It is not for him either a toy or, despite
his love of ostentation, a costly and fragile object of luxury; it is a
useful tool, an indispensable companion in that life of action, struggle,
and adventure which he loves because such a life is independent,
"blessed by God and far from the sultans."

It can be understood that this second part of my study, each part
having the horse as its objective, must, nonetheless, differ essentially
from the first.[1] Now the horse has reached its full development, all
its forces are at work—it has received its obligatory complement,

[1] A reference to General Daumas's study of the native (Barb) horse of Algeria.
The work has been translated into English by Sheila M. Ohlendorf and published
under the title *The Horses of the Sahara*. [Translator's note]

the horseman. From that moment they lead a life so straitly joined
that I cannot neglect the one upon occupying myself with the other.
I am then obliged to introduce Arab ways fully at a time (1850)
in our [French] history wherein the excesses of force do not at
all prevent a noble and touching practice of devotion, bravery, and
courtesy.

Chivalry, in the full sense of the term, with all its adventures, is
the usual life of the Arab of the desert; I mean that of the noble,
of the master of the tent. All the rest is chance or is naught but
the lot of him who lodges in the *kuesours* (villages), of the lower-
class townsman, of the laborer, palmgrower, merchant, domestic,
or shepherd.

It is of the life of adventure that I am going to give a rough
outline.

OBSERVATIONS OF THE EMIR ABD-EL-KADER

It is true that the Arabs have been the most experienced horsemen
of the world, knowing the horse down to the least detail and knowing
how to breed and train it better than any other people. It is also true
that Arabian horses are better runners than all the horses of other nations. A sufficient proof, in that regard, is that they wind up by over-
taking the gazelle, the ostrich, the wild ass, in whose pursuit they
sometimes start from very far away.

*He has hunted the onager, the wild ox and the ostrich in one burst,
without one drop of sweat having dampened his coat.*

The temperament of the horses of the Sahara is a consequence of the
life of their masters. It is very necessary that the Saharians accustom
their horses to withstand hunger, because of the scarcity of feed, and
thirst, because of the scarcity of water, which often is not found but
at one or two days' journey from their encampment. Speed and resistance to fatigue come from the innumerable quarrels among these
Arabs, from their incursions of incessant war, from their taste for the
chase of the swiftest animals [such as] the ostrich, the gazelle, the
onager—a chase which certain from among them make all year long
without interruption.

The Almighty has said: "Place then in readiness all the forces of

which you dispose and have horses ready in great numbers to intimi-
date God's enemies and your own and yet others whom you do not
know but whom God knows. All that which you might have expended
on God's ways shall be repaid to you and you will not be left."

And the Prophet has not ceased to repeat:

> He who owns an Arabian horse and honors him,
> God shall honor him.
> He who owns an Arabian horse and disdains him,
> God shall disdain him.

THE SAHARA

by the Emir Abd-el-Kader

The dwellers in houses are, everywhere, forced to acknowledge a master; whereas we, always as ready for combat as for flight, do not acknowledge any master other than God.

GLORY TO GOD ALONE

O You! who take the side of the *hader*[1]
And condemn the love of the *bedoui*[2]
For his limitless horizons!
Is it for their lightness
That you reproach our tents?
Have you eulogies only
For houses of mud and stone?
If you knew the secrets of the desert,
You would think as I do;
But you are unaware of them and
Ignorance is the mother of evil.

If you had been bred in the midst of the Sahara;
If your feet had trodden that carpet of sand

---

[1] *Hader:* townsman.
[2] *Bedoui:* dweller in the wastes of the Sahara.

Strewn with flowers resembling pearls,
You would have admired our plants;
The strange variety of their hues,
Their grace, their delicious perfume.

You would have breathed that embalméd air
Which renews life
For it has not passed over the impurities of towns.
If, upon going out on a splendid night,
Refreshed by an abundant dew,
From the top of a *merkeb*[3]
You had gazed about you,
You would have seen, in the distance,
Everywhere troops of wild animals
Browsing on the aromatic bushes.
At that hour all care would have fled before you;
An abundant joy would have filled your soul.

What delights [there are] also in our hunts!
At the rising of the sun, because of us,
Each day brings fear to the wild animal.

And on the day of the *rahil*[4]
When our red *haouadjej*[5] are girthed on the camels,
You would think it a field of anemones,
Deepening, in the rain, their richest tones.

On our *haouadjej* lie virgins.
Their *taka*[6] are shut by the eyes of *houris*.[7]
The camel drivers make their shrill cries heard;
The timbre of their voices finds the portal of the soul.

We, swift as the air on our generous coursers,
Chelils floating over their croups,[8]

---

3 *Merkeb:* in the Sahara, the name given to a hillock whose appearance calls to mind the shape of a ship.
4 *Rahil:* migration, nomadic movement.
5 *Haouadjej:* camel litters.
6 *Taka:* windows, peepholes in the litters.
7 *Houris:* nymphs of the Mohammedan paradise, supposed to be created from musk and spices and endowed with perpetually virgin youth and perfect beauty. [Translator's note]
8 *Chelil:* housing floating over the horse's croup, made of silk and worn on festive occasions.

Pursue the *houache*.[9]
We overtake the *ghrezal*[10]
Who thought itself far from us.
(But) it does not escape our trained horses
With their slender flanks.
How many *délim* and their mates
Have not been our victims![11]
Granted that their speed
Does not concede anything
To the flight of other birds.

We return to our families at the hour when the convoy halts
On a new camping ground, free from all impurity.
The earth breathes musk,[12]
But, purer than it, it has been bleached by
The evening and morning rains.

We erect our tents in circular groups.
The earth is covered with them as the firmament with stars.
The ancients have said—they are no longer more—
But our fathers have repeated to us
And we say as they do,
For truth is ever truth:
Two things are beautiful in the world,
Beautiful verse and lovely tents.

In the evening our camels draw close to us;
At night the voice of the male is like distant thunder.
Swift ships of the land, surer than ships,
For the ship is inconstant,
Our *maharis*[13] rival the *maha*[14] in swiftness.

And, our horses. Is there an equal glory?
Always saddled for combat.
For whomsoever demands our aid,
They are the promise of victory.

---

[9] *Houache:* a species of bison or wild ox.
[10] *Ghrezal:* gazelle.
[11] *Délim:* male ostrich.
[12] The scent of musk remains where the gazelle has passed.
[13] *Maharis:* racing camels.
[14] *Maha:* a kind of wild white doe.

Our enemies have no refuge against our coups,
For our coursers, celebrated by the Prophet,[15]
Fall on them like the vulture.

Our coursers are given the purest of milk to drink;
It is camel's milk, more precious than that of the cow.
The first of our cares is to share the booty taken
    from the enemy.
Justice prevails over the sharing; each receives the
    price of his bravery.

We have sold our right to the city;
We have nothing to regret in our bargain.
We have gained honor, the *hader* knows it not.
Kings we are; nothing can be compared with us.
Is it living to suffer humiliation?
We do not tolerate the affront of the unjust;
We leave him, him and his land.
True good fortune lies in the nomadic life.

If association with a neighbor hampers us,
We withdraw from him.
Neither he, nor we, have any complaint.

With what then can you reproach the *bedoui?*
Nothing but his love of glory
And his generosity which knows no bounds.
Under the tent the fire of hospitality
Glows for the traveler.
He finds, no matter who he might be,
An assured haven against hunger and cold.

Time has stated the salubrity of the Sahara.
All the sick, all the infirm
Dwell only under the roofs of towns.
In the Sahara he, whom steel has not harvested,
Sees days without limit.
Our graybeards are the oldest of all men.

---

15 An allusion to the *sourate* (chapters) of the Koran.

3

RAZZIAS (FORAYS)

> I have surprised them with purebred horses,
> with their foreheads adorned with a star,
> portent of good luck, with flanks made slen-
> der by hunting, with hard firm flesh and
> falling on them like the cloud charged with
> lightning which covers a gorge.

The most frequent and almost daily deed in Arab life is the *razzia*. Glory is a beautiful thing, no doubt, to which the heart is sensitive in the Sahara, as it is everywhere, furthermore. But there [in the Sahara] glory is held as doing harm to the enemy, destroying his resources, upon augmenting one's own. Glory does not lie in smoke, but in plunder. A desire for vengeance is also a motive, but is there a more beautiful vengeance than that of enriching oneself from the spoils of the enemy?

That threefold desire for glory, vengeance, and plunder cannot find a more expeditious or effective procedure to satisfy itself than the *razzia*, an incursion by force or ruse of the spot occupied by the enemy, of the storehouse of all that he holds dear—family and fortune.

In the desert the *razzias* are of three kinds: First there is the *téhha* (literally the *falling upon,* from the verb *tahh,* he is fallen). It is done at daybreak *(fedjeur).* In a *téhha* one has not come to plunder, one is aroused to massacre, one does not enrich oneself, one takes revenge.

Then there is the *khrotefa,* which takes place at *el àasseur,* at two or three o'clock in the afternoon. It is rapine.

Lastly there is the *terbigue.* It is not war, it is not an attack by a bandit or a brigand, it is scarcely more than a thief's trick at the most. The *terbigue* is done at *nous el leïl,* midnight.

When a *razzia* has been decided upon, those who are to take part in it say among themselves: *rana akeud,* we are *bound.* An undertaking is arranged, the association is formed—the pact is concluded—a pact of life and death.

El téhha (The falling upon)

The *téhha* is planned, the sheik gives the order to shoe the horses, prepare the rations, lay in a stock of barley for five or six days more or less. These rations are carried in saddlebags, *semmâte,* for each his own.

Before starting off, two or four mounted *chouafin* (scouts) are sent to reconnoiter the emplacement of the tribe to be attacked. These scouts are intelligent, alert, well mounted, and they know the country-side. They travel with great precaution, make a wide detour, and, in case of surprise, will present themselves on the side from which the tribe to be attacked ordinarily does not see other than friends appear. Arrived close to their goal, they go into hiding. One of them detaches himself and on foot penetrates as far as the midst of the *douars,*[1] without exciting the least suspicion. Once the forces and disposition of the enemy have been reconnoitered, the scouts retrace their steps and go to rejoin the *goum,*[2] who are waiting for them at a predetermined place and who, like the scouts, have followed a line of country in such a manner as not to inspire any fear in those whom it is desired to surprise. All the details are collected, the camp to be invaded is very close; it is necessary to fall upon it at daybreak, for at that hour are found:

> *El mera bela hazame,*
> *Ou el aouda bela ledjame.*

> (The woman without her girdle
> And the mare without her bridle.)

[1] *Douars:* a subdivision of a tribe is called a *douar* (circle). The tents are pitched in a circle and it is from that that the name is derived. [Translator's note]
[2] *Goum:* a troop of horsemen of a tribe, or a fraction of a tribe, armed for war [Translator's note]

Before hurling themselves into that melee the chieftains address a
fiery speech to their horsemen: "Pay attention! Let not one of you
think of ravishing women, carrying off horses, entering tents, or dismounting to pick up booty, before having done a great deal of killing.
Remember what we have to do to those *sons of sin,* who will defend
themselves vigorously. Those people massacred our brothers. No quarter—kill, kill!—if you wish to have both vengeance and the enemy's
goods, for, I repeat, he will not yield the latter to you at a bargain
price."

Then the *goum* divides into three or four bodies to throw terror into
the tribe from many sides at the same time. As soon as one has come
within range, fire is opened; no shouting as long as the gunpowder has
not yet made itself heard.

These *razzias,* most of the time, turn into shocking carnages. The
men, caught unawares, are almost all put to death; it is enough to
despoil the women of their garments. If time permits, the victors carry
off the tents, lead away the Negroes, the horses, the herds. The women
and children are abandoned. In the desert one never burdens oneself
with prisoners. On the return, the herds are placed under the guard of
some horsemen and a strong reserve is formed, charged with parrying
all eventualities on withdrawal.

Returned to the *douar* the warriors share among themselves the herds
and all booty taken without risk to life; they give, over and above, to
the sheik thirty or forty sheep and three or four she-camels, according
to circumstances; and they reward in a special manner the horsemen
who had gone on ahead as scouts.

Before attempting an enterprise of that nature each tribe places itself
under the protection of a particular Marabout (holy man) to whom the
tribe addresses itself in trying circumstances. What I have said at the
head of this chapter will make it understood that, for the Saharian, the
pillaging of an enemy is an event which, despite what it contains of
habitualness, does not lack solemnity. It is thus that the tribe of the
Arbâa has, as an incumbent Marabout, Sidi Hamed-ben-Salem Ould
Tedjiny.

The success of a *razzia* is an occasion for great rejoicing; in each tent
an *ouadâa* (fête) is prepared in honor of the Marabouts and the poor,

the *tolbas* (scribes), the widows, the farriers,[3] and the free Negroes are invited.

The *téhha* is customarily carried out with five or six hundred horse; often infantry, transported on camelback, is added.

Sometimes the tribe which it is desired to attack has been warned in time and takes its own measures. The horses are saddled, the arms readied, there is combat and not slaughter. Many horsemen are killed on both sides, but the attackers almost always have the advantage. They are not encumbered with women and children as are their enemies; it is rare that they return without booty.

I believe I should set forth here one of the popular songs which so well depict the ardor and the moving scenes of these bloody struggles of which love and jealousy are but all too frequently the causes in the Sahara:

My horse is whiter than the snow;
Whiter than men's shrouds;
He bounds like the gazelle
And bears me toward your father's tent.

O Yamina![4] Mad are they who feed your pride;
Even madder are they who tell me to forget you.
I would I were the clasp of your *haïk*;[5]
A lock of your black hair;
The *meroueud* which darkens your eyes,[6]
Or, better yet, the carpet you tread under your feet.

I watered my horse at the fountainhead,[7]

---

[3] The farriers of Arab tribes were held in great esteem and did not go to war. Their lives were generally spared and the tools of their trade returned to them if their tribe was attacked. [Translator's note]

[4] Yamina: a feminine proper name very common among the Arabs.

[5] "The clasp of your *haïk*": the women use a large silver clasp to fasten their *haïk*, a long piece of woolen stuff in which they envelop themselves. That clasp, in the desert, bears the name of *khelala*.

[6] *Meroueud:* a small sliver of polished wood which the women use to put on their eyelids that antimony (*koheul*) they regard so highly.

[7] "At the fountainhead": an expression depicting the care with which the Arabs choose the water they give their horses. It can be imagined that the water is always purer at the fountainhead than farther downstream, where it might have been roiled. Because many streams and watering places in Algeria are heavily infested by leeches, the Arabs exercise great vigilance over the water their animals are given to drink. [Translator's note]

Then I leapt lightly on his back.
My *chabir* adhere to his flanks,[8]
And I have faith in my weapons as I have faith in my heart;
They have betrayed me for the moon of my soul,[9]
The days will betray them also.

For God or the vultures!
Why do you plane through the skies?
I ask God that he give us one of those bloody combats
Wherein each can die with his flesh and not from a sickness.[10]
You will spend the days and nights feasting!
Our lives and those of our horses
Do they not belong to the young girls?

Be gone, strangers, be gone!
Leave the flowers of our meadows
For the bees of our land.
Be gone, strangers, be gone!

O the generous one!
You see her then this night
Where our *goums* were able to hurl gunpowder
As far as the *douar* of Yamina,
While the women there were still without a belt[11]
And the horses were in iron hobbles[12]
Before the *aâtatouche*[13] have been placed on the camels' backs
And before the horsemen have pulled on their *temag*[14]
Cause that I receive seven balls in my burnoose,
Seven in my horse

[8] "To his flanks": Arab spurs (*chabir*), because of their length, can only be placed lengthwise on the horse's barrel or flanks.
[9] "The moon of my soul": Arab poets have a custom of comparing the women of whom they speak to the moon. The moon, they say, shines with a softer light than that of the sun; it announces calm freshness and predisposes to romantic reveries.
[10] "Die with his flesh": the poet wishes to say, "die in a combat, full of health and strength and not wasted by misery or old age."
[11] "Without a belt": every Arab woman wears a wide belt, or girdle. She removes it at night to put it on again at daybreak.
[12] In the Sahara thefts are so frequent that during the night iron hobbles are put on all the horses.
[13] *Aâtatouche:* a kind of chair, more or less ornate according to the means of the individual, placed on camels' backs and in which the Arab women sit when they have to travel.
[14] *Temag:* boots made of red morocco leather called *filaly*.

And that I may have placed seven in the body of my rival.[15]
The best of loves is that which makes the teeth clench.

Fly, young men, fly![16]
Balls do not kill.
It is only Destiny that kills.
Fly, young men, fly!

Kaddour's horse is dead, Kaddour's horse is dead!
Publish it among your tribes, they will be rejoiced about it;
But, if you are not Jews,[17] add that,
Bleeding and wounded, he was able to save his master
And extricate him from the encounter;
It was that he did not wish to give the lie to his forebears.[18]
He, who had not been trained for flight,
He, who did not know how to gallop but to clash;
Merouan died for Yamina, his days were numbered!

O my heart!
Why are you set upon making the waters rise toward the mountains?
You are the fool who pursues the sun!
Believe me!
Cease to love a woman who will never say yes to you.
Seed sown in a *sebkha* will never produce shoots.[19]

---

15 "Seven balls in the body of my rival": there are many Arabs who, for combat, load their rifles with seven balls or shot, with *hamous*; but their arms in general being poor and badly kept, that custom becomes the source of a host of accidents. The number of persons maimed by rifle barrels exploding in their hands is considerable. I knew in the province of Oran a chieftain of the Bordjias, named Kaddour-ben-Mokhfy, who had the reputation of having killed, during his life, a large number of individuals. An admirable horseman, always superiorly mounted, he loaded his rifle with seven balls or shot and when, in a line of snipers he had, with an eagle glance, perceived a foolhardy enemy who, upon advancing, had committed the error of discharging his fire, he hurled himself upon him with such swiftness that he had usually overtaken and thrown him to the ground, him or his horse, before his comrades could come to his aid. Kaddour-ben-Mokhfy is still, at the time I write, our Agha of the Bordjias.

16 "Fly," in this sense, means urge your horses to their greatest speed.

17 "Jews": an expression of disdain of which the Arabs make daily use to prick the self-esteem of their interlocutors.

18 "To give the lie": rightly or wrongly, the Arabs are convinced that a purebred horse, even if mortally wounded, will still find strength enough not to leave his master in the power of the enemy.

19 *Sebkha:* a salty terrain which can furnish salt but is resistant to any form of agricultural cultivation.

El Khrotefa (Rapine)

The object of the *razzia* called *el khrotefa* is the carrying-off of a herd of camels grazing seven or eight leagues from the tribe [which owns it]. One hundred and fifty to two hundred horsemen join in *akeud* (bond) and start off. Reconnaissance is made, as in the *téhha,* but arrangements are made with a view to arriving at the place where the coup is to be carried out toward *el àasseur* (three or four o'clock in the afternoon) and not toward *fedjeur* (daybreak).

The *razzia* performed, three, four, or six *ybal* (a troop of one hundred she-camels) carried off, two groups are formed. One, composed of the weakest horses, takes the lead with the booty; the other forms a kind of rearguard, charged with resisting the enemy. The groups separate after having agreed upon a rendezvous for the following day at a set point. But, in order to mislead the pursuers better, the group which is to halt the enemy follows a different road from that of the conductors of the lifted herds.

In these coups the shepherds are generally spared. Moreover, it is unusual that they defend possessions which do not belong to them.

But soon noise—shouts of all kinds—gives the alarm. Each saddles his horse and launches himself. Then a halt is made, it is necessary to rally, and finally numbers of men present themselves on the spot. This time the assailants still have every favorable chance; they are on the alert, ready to take on the enemy, their horses have had time to rest. Those of the pillaged tribe are harassed, blown. A fusillade begins at once, but night falls. As soon as it deepens, "when the eye begins to darken," the ravishers break off and at a gallop go to rejoin the other group, which they encounter at sunrise.

They have been pursued for but a short time. The conviction that its camels are out of reach, the fear of ambush, soon make the tribe return to its tents.

Although the combat which accompanies this kind of expedition is not, in general, very lively, and is very soon cut short by nightfall, those who take part in it run risks, nonetheless. A horseman can receive a grave wound which renders him unfit to continue traveling. He is lost, if he is not a person of distinction. In that case he would never be abandoned. A sturdy horseman would take charge of him, lay him across his own saddle and take him with him, dead or alive. With respect to slight wounds, with an Arabian saddle these are of no great moment and do not prevent the rejoining of the *goum*.

Upon reentry into the *douars* the booty is shared among those who took part in the *khrotefa*.

El Terbigue (Theft)

For the *terbigue* only fifteen or twenty horsemen, who are *akeud* (bound), propose to carry off herds from the very midst of some *douar*. They send *chouafin* (scouts) to reconnoiter the tribe and arrive close to the tents on the darkest of nights.

An isolated *douar* is chosen and it is approached to within a distance of two or three hundred paces. Three men dismount and halt. One of them detaches himself, goes to the opposite side and makes a noise to attract the dogs.

"It is a hyena or a jackal out there," the people of the *douar* think to themselves and during those moments do not go on guard. The other two thieves enter the interior of the *douar,* untie the hobbles of ten, fifteen, or twenty camels, according to how much or how little safety there is, take their slippers, slap them against each other, frightening the freed animals and making them run away.

Those who have carried out the coup withdraw as speedily as possible. Their horses are brought and together they round up the dispersed camels. Then they separate into two bands; one is in charge of carrying off the prize, while the other, delaying a little while, causes itself to be pursued in another direction. If it has succeeded in freeing the *faâla* (the sire camel), the coup is a most fortunate one, for all the females seek to follow their male.

The secret of these coups de main is generally well kept; it is rare that they fail. Accidents are not very frequent. When the *douar* is on the alert, the thieves withdraw. Those who take chances in such enterprises generally have good horses and swiftly elude pursuit, which, moreover, is next to impossible at night, when traces are easily lost or ambushes are to be feared. For a *razzia* of this kind there is no hesitation in doing thirty or forty leagues.

Sometimes the *terbigue* is complicated by ludicrous incidents. A party of horsemen, not wishing to leave a reserve to combat the enemy in case of need, goes into hiding at seven or eight hundred paces from the *douar*. The most adroit thief strips himself naked, keeping only his saber, and ties his slippers about his head like huge ears. Thus accoutered he bursts into the *douar,* having in his hand a battered saddletree, which he waves about in all directions and with which he strikes the ground from time to time. To that dull sound he adds cries of fright and alarm:

"Here's the *goum!* See the *goum!* Up! To us, we are sold!"

The clamor, the gamboling, the strange aspect of that naked figure, the movement and the noise of the saddletree which he waves about strike terror into the herds: horses, sheep, camels break loose, make for the open, and are herded together by the hidden horsemen.

Men fling out of the tents, take arms, mount horses; but the thief is in the saddle, herds and marauders are far away, fleeing at top speed and protected by the night.

4

KHRIANA (ROBBERY)

O Sidi Abd-el-Kader! Thou who art the patron of all those who are in misery, save us this time yet once again and, upon our return, we will give in thy honor an *ouadâa* (a feast for the poor).

El khriana is a robbery but, furthermore, it is almost war; it is the *razzia*. The number of men who carry out the enterprise, the importance of the theft executed by a fraction of an entire tribe, the quality of the partisans who go on campaign and who, after all, are horsemen—that is to say, warriors—all these circumstances, if they are not excuses to our eyes, to us, scrupulous Europeans, are very plausible motives in the desert. Brave outposts have risked themselves to injure an enemy tribe. There cannot but be joy and triumph in that of which they form a part.

We shall go one degree lower, where we reach pure marauding, executed by professional thieves. In it there is no longer war, even attenuated. It is theft, plain and simple. It is not a subject for rejoicing by an entire tribe, but it is, nonetheless, a matter for praise and congratulations among friends, always on the condition that the robbery has not been committed within the tribe itself or within an allied tribe. Such robbery would be a dishonor. But when it is from an enemy it is said: "So-and-so is a brave man. He robs from the enemy."

As can easily be imagined, not all robberies are carried out in the same manner and the means used are appropriate for the type of capture in mind.

Theft of Horses

This type of theft is carried out toward the end of the Moslem month when the moon is barely visible; five or six men in full agreement carry rations (*rouina*) in sacks called *mezoueud* and start off seeking adventure.

Before departure they give alms (*el mâarouf*) to the poor and pray them to intercede with God for the success of the enterprise, then they swear by a known Marabout, most often Sidi Abd-el-Kader, to pay him homage;[1] in case of success, of a share (*mezerague*), which will be distributed to the unfortunate.

"O Sidi Abd-el-Kader!" they say, "if we return joyous, with booty and without accident, we shall give thee, if it please God, thy lance [*mezerague*]."

Upon leaving the *douar* the thieves travel in full daylight. When they approach the tribe from which they have the intention of stealing, they travel only at night and go into hiding at two or three leagues from the tents, in a riverbed, in the grasses (*alfa*), or on the mountain. As soon as the night has become very dark they leave their hiding place, investigate all the *douars*, one after another, and halt at the one where the guard seems to be the least active or where the dogs appear to be least alert.

If the thieves are six in number, four remain some fifty paces from the *douar*, immobile and silent. The other two, the boldest and most adroit, penetrate into the interior. On separating they give each other a countersign (*mana*).

The two thieves set about their task. If they find the dogs on the alert they return to add a third companion whom they place a short distance in front of the tent where the dogs are so vigilant. They then enter the *douar* from another side. They point out the tent which they wish to rob. Then one of them, called the *gaad*, remains as a sentinel close to it, and the other, *el hammaze*, draws close to the

---

[1] The Marabout referred to here is Sidi Abd-el-Kader-el-Djelali of Baghdad, of the oldest of the Mohammedan brotherhoods.

horses. *El hammaze*, if he finds a mare or a horse hobbled only with leather straps or with ropes, unties or cuts them, catches hold of the animal by the *goulada* (a cord hung with talismans placed around the neck), and leads it off on the opposite side from that where the dogs are busy for the time being with the *layahh*.[2]

The *gaad* remains behind, ready to kill with a single shot or to bludgeon with a club or a stone the first person who emerges from the tent, and ready to mislead others by taking a direction different from that taken by his comrade who led off the horse. Then the *gaad* rejoins the *layahh* and they quickly rejoin *el hammaze* and the three companions who are waiting for them.

The theft is renewed if the *douar*, plunged in sleep, has not noted anything, but, if not, it is decided to depart. One of the thieves, placing his folded *haïk* on the horse's back in such a way as to form stirrups, departs at a gallop after having made a rendezvous with his companions at an agreed-upon site, for the following day or the day after that. The others, to evade the pursuit which would be made in the morning, hide all during the first night. He who rides the stolen horse does not continue his route except in the case wherein the theft was committed during the first hours of night; if not, he spends all of the next day hidden in a dry and rocky place where the animal leaves no trace.

If, instead of being rope, the hobbles are of iron, the operation becomes more complicated. The preliminaries are the same, but once at work *el hammaze* carefully raises the hobbles as far as the knees, keeps them in place with a camelhide thong tied around the neck, and makes the animal walk with mincing steps. As soon as he rejoins his comrades and as soon as he as far enough away from the *douar*, victim of the theft, he longs to give his prize the freedom it lacks. He then removes the hobbles by means of a small saw (*cherrima*) or a hook. If worst comes to worst he pulls the padlock to the outside of the horse's legs and breaks it with a pistol shot or fills it with gunpowder and blows it up.

But the detonation awakens the masters of the horse; they go in

---

2 *Layahh:* entertainer, he who distracts attention. It is the name given to the third companion remaining in front of the tent because of the dogs.

search of it, almost always in vain; the night is dark and the thieves divide. As a last resort they get out of the difficulty by abandoning the prize to save their lives.

Sometimes the master of the tent is astonished by the barking of the dogs. He wakes everyone up, he shouts: "There is someone about! (*El hayi rah hena!*)."

He emerges, finds nothing, persuades himself that it was a jackal or a hyena that occasioned all that noise and goes back to sleep. The thieves reappear or go toward another *douar* which is less well guarded.

When preparations are being made for a *khriana* one should be furnished with a pistol which is placed under the burnoose, a knife, a bludgeon having a rope at one end, and a dagger (*seboula*). If a thief thinks that the dogs will distinguish him because of the whiteness of his garments, he leaves them with his comrades and penetrates the *douar* completely naked, knife in one hand, bludgeon in the other. It is a popular belief in the Sahara that a completely naked man is not visible on a dark night.

Never is an attempt made to steal a very vicious or purebred horse or one that is used for stud. The neighing of those animals at the sight of the man would betray the robber.

To avoid being sensed by the dogs care is taken to move against the wind. Other weather conditions should not be neglected, the absence of a moon, for instance. It is necessary to start off on the twenty-first of the Moslem month and the night of the twenty-second is customarily the most favorable time. Dust and high wind are useful auxiliaries, but rain is a traitor. It drenches the ground, which retains tracks; it favors pursuit.

The cold season is the good one for the thefts of which we are speaking. It is commonly said on that subject: "In winter the thefts of livestock, because the dog sleeps in the tent—in summer thefts inside the tent, for then the dog goes far away to sleep."

Like every other Arab, the thief believes that God would not disdain to warn him. From that [belief] stem hopes and superstitious fears. For instance, if, upon departure from the *douar*, he encounters a black, dirty, lean mare, in poor condition, in other words, [it is] a sad omen (*fal chine*) and he turns back. If he hears himself, at the moment of departure, being called by people who do not know where he is going [it is] another bad portent (*el nechâa*). To see two partridges, a good augury; one only, a disagreeable prognostication. If he encounters, upon departure, a lighthearted, courageous, well-dressed, and well-mounted man, infallible success. An old woman, blind or crippled, covered with rags, will infallibly prevent success. But he departs with all confidence if he has encountered a lovely woman, richly dressed, to whom he has said: "Open thy belt, Fatma, it will bring us good luck." She will not refuse to open to him the door of riches. It is equally desirable to see along the way a woman carrying milk and to take a swallow of it.

Upon their return, the thieves make a division. The vow made to the Marabouts they invoked is scrupulously fulfilled; the chieftain of their *douar*, the woman who untied her belt—each receives a gift. The share that falls to *el hammaze* is much larger. It is he, it will be remembered, who has played the most important role and run the greatest dangers.

Theft of Camels

The theft of camels is carried out in the same way as that of horses. Choice falls upon made camels, that is to say, those which no longer cry out, or pregnant she-camels.

The hobbles removed, the thieves goad the animal with a dagger or knife to make it leave and mount it once they are at a great distance from the tents. They travel all night. If at daybreak it is considered that they are not far enough away to escape pursuit by the horsemen, a halt is made and they hide in a place where the ground will not retain tracks. The horsemen give up the pursuit when they do not find anything. If not, they often recover that which was stolen from them, and the thieves, unless they have let go their prize and are not ambushed, pay for their enterprise with their lives.[3]

It is the supreme moment of invocations and vows.

---

[3] Among certain tribes of the desert the thief caught *in flagrante delicto* is covered, as if clothed from top to toe, with *alfa* (esparto grass) and set on fire. The wretched man is then released and, pursued by a general hue and cry, goes off to die of burns a little farther on.

"O Sidi Abd-el-Kader!" exclaims the thief who feels the enemy close to him and trembles for fear of being discovered, "if thou wilt save us this time yet once again, we will give in thy honor an *ouadâa* for the poor."

In the Sahara, Sidi Abd-el-Kader Djelaly is the patron of thieves. That disreputable following is explained by the charity of the saintly Marabout who does not wish to leave in misery any one of those who invoke his name.

Theft of Sheep

Sheep are a slender booty and one that is more of a hindrance than it is profitable. They are animals that travel slowly and desperate efforts must be made to conduct them to a great enough distance the day after the theft. Thus it is enough to maraud from the enemy, when he is absent, the mutton necessary to live on in ambuscades.

Sometimes, however, the opportunity is tempting. The flock is seen grazing far from the *douars*. The shepherd is lying down, asleep or distracted in some way. It is late in the morning, there is time to cover ground before the setting of the sun, the hour for the return of the flocks. The *douars* will be unaware of the theft which has been committed; the coup is hazarded.

The negligent shepherd is given a vigorous blow on the head with a club, sand is thrown in his eyes, he is covered with his *guelmouna* (the hood of the burnoose), his hands are tied behind his back and the thieves share the driving of the flock, divided into small lots. Each follows a separate path, slowly at first and then more quickly. The following day, after having traveled only through uninhabited places, they reunite at a designated spot. The shepherd is taken along and he is not released until the middle of the night when there is no longer anything to be feared from him.

5

WAR AMONG THE TRIBES OF THE DESERT

> Fly, young men, fly!
> Balls do not kill,
> It is only Destiny that kills.
> Fly, young men, fly!

A caravan has been pillaged, the women of the tribe have been out-raged, there has been a struggle over water and grazing grounds. Behold that for those grievances the *razzia,* be it the terrible *téhha,* is not sufficient vengeance. The chieftains have gathered and have de-creed war.

They have written to all the chieftains of allied tribes and have de-manded their aid. The allies are faithful and sure; do they not also have the enemies of the tribe to punish? Do they not have the same sympathies, the same interests as those who summon them? Do they not form part of the *soff,* of the rank, of the confederation? Not one of the tribes will refuse to send its contingent in proportion to its importance.

But the allies are far away. They cannot arrive before [the lapse of] eight or ten days. While waiting, councils are renewed and the chief-tains inflame spirits by their proclamations:

"You are warned, O slaves of God, that we must exact vengeance from such and such a tribe, which has offered us such and such an affront! Shoe your horses, lay in provisions for fifteen days. Do not forget wheat, barley, dried meat (*khreléa*), and butter. You should provide not only for your own needs, but also in order to be able to accord hospitality generously to the horsemen of such and such and such tribes who are coming to our support. Order your prettiest women to be ready to march with us, to ornament themselves with their most beautiful garb, to caparison with their best their camels and their *aâtatouche* [parade palanquins]. You, yourselves, wear your richest garments, as for us this is a matter of *nif* [amour propre]. Have your arms in good condition, supply yourselves with gunpowder, and be gathered, on such and such a day, at such and such a spot. The horseman who has a mare and does not come, the infantryman who has a rifle and remains behind, will be penalized, the first with a fine of twenty ewes and the second with a fine of ten ewes. Every able-bodied man, even if afoot, should form part of the expedition."

It is time for departure, but first the chieftains entrust the flocks and herds, the tents, and the baggage of the tribe to the care of experienced graybeards, also charged with acting as police and with the surveillance of that gathering of women, children, invalids, and shepherds.

The enemies have also made their preparations. Warned by travelers, friends, even by the relatives they have in the opposing party, they hasten to write everywhere to rally their allies (their *soff*). They place the herds, the tents, and the baggage in a place they believe to be safe, then a rendezvous is assigned to the horsemen with the least possible delay. Because of the fear of a surprise, a terrain suitable for defense is chosen and developments are awaited.

Events are imminent and the tribe which has taken up arms to avenge itself is going to start off very soon—it has not lost a moment. On the eve of departure all the allied chieftains join those who sent for them. In the presence of the Marabouts they swear on the Holy Book of Sidi-Abd-Allah the following oath: "O our friends! We swear by the truth of the Holy Book of Sidi-Abd-Allah that we are brothers, that we will not be but one and the same rifle and that, should we die, we will all die from the same saber. If you summon us by day, we will come by day and if you call us by night, we will come by night."

The participants, after having sworn, agree to depart the following morning.

The next day at the appointed hour a man of high birth, a noble (*djieud*)[1] among the most noble, mounts his horse, causes his women, borne by camels, to follow him, and gives the signal. Then all quivers, all is set in motion. The eye is dazzled by that strange and picturesque horde, that motley throng of horses and warriors—and camels bearing the ornate palanquins in which the women are enclosed.

Here are the infantrymen, who form a separate band; there, the horsemen who keep watch over the women's travel. Others, more fiery, more high-spirited, have gone on ahead or scatter themselves along the flanks, less as scouts than as hunters. With their salukis they flush the gazelle, hare, antelope, or ostrich. The chieftains are graver; on them rests the responsibility. It is to them that the greatest share of the booty will fall if the expedition succeeds, but, if there is a reverse, for them imprecations, ruin, and dishonor. They confer among themselves and ponder.

Then come the camels carrying the provisions.

All that throng, conforming to the demands of the terrain, all that disorderly, noisy, and joyous throng dreams of adventure, not fatigue; of glory, not perils. The warriors vaunt their exploits of all kinds; the flute players accompany, enliven, or interrupt them. The women utter shrieks of joy. Those sounds are dominated by the intoxicating bursts of gunpowder.

Then the rifles fall silent. A young and handsome horseman begins one of those love songs which passion takes pleasure in strewing with dazzling colors and strange imagery and which, in the desert, always have a new charm for those chivalresque peoples:

> My heart burns with its fire
> For a woman come from Paradise.

[1] *Djieud:* a noble; plural, *djouad:* among the Arabs the names *djieud* and *djouad* are given to the military nobility. They derive their origin from the Méhal, conquerors come from the East on the heels of the companions of the Prophet. The common man has much to bear from the injustices and spoliations of the *djouad*. The latter seek to cause these mistreatments to be forgotten and would maintain their influence by according their hospitality and protection generously to those who

O! You who do not know Meryem[2]
That marvel of the only God,
I shall show you her portrait.
Meryem is the bey Osman himself
When he appears with his standards,
The drums that roar
And his *goums* which follow him.

Meryem is a purebred mare
Who lives with delights
In a gilded palace;
She loves the shade of the leaves,
She drinks a limpid water
And desires Blacks to attend her.

Meryem is the moon of the stars
Which betrays the thieves[3]
Or rather, she is moreover the palm
Of the land of the Beni-Mzab[4]
Whose fruit is so high
It cannot be touched.

Meryem is rather the gazelle
When it runs in the desert.
The hunter places its little one at stake.
It sees the fuse burn,
Knows how to receive the blow
And die to save its life.

She has given me a rendezvous
For the night of Monday.
My heart beats. She is come!
All enveloped in silk,

---

ask it; that is to say, they join, to a supreme degree, the two salient traits of national character: avidity and a great love of luxury.

[2] Mary.

[3] "Which betrays the thieves": Arab thieves rarely start off when the moon is full. It has been noted that there are many more thefts and assassinations in Arab countries at the end of the lunar month.

[4] The Beni-Mzab: in the midst of the populations of the desert, a small people, apart, distinguished by the severity of its customs, its particular tongue, its proverbial probity, and some modifications in religious practices. It is a confederation and numbers seven important towns of which the principal one is Ghardaïa.

She throws herself into my arms.
Meryem has no sister[5]
In the four corners of the world!

She is worth Tunis with Algiers,
Tlemsen, and Mascara,
Their shops and markets
And their perfumed materials.

She is worth the ships
Which cross the blue[6] with their sails
To seek the riches
Which God has created for us.[7]

She is worth five hundred mares,
The fortune of a tribe
When they gallop toward the gunpowder
Under their proud riders.

She is worth five hundred she-camels
Followed by their little ones,
More than one hundred Negroes of the Sudan
Stolen by the Tuareg[8] to serve the Moslems.

She is worth all the nomadic Arabs,
Happy, independent;
And those with fixed dwellings,
Unfortunate victims
Of the caprice of the sultans.[9]

---

5 "Meryem has no sister": a consecrated expression in the arabic tongue to say: "she has no equal."

6 "The blue": *zerga*, here, means the sea.

7 "Which God has created for us": here is revealed in all its strength the Arab's pride. With the produce from our horses, our camels, and our sheep, they say, we have no need to work. We can, however, procure for ourselves everything that is manufactured, with such toil, by those wretched Christians..

8 "Stolen by the Touareg (or Tuareg)": a large tribe, of Berber origin, which guards the gates of the Sahara and the Sudan, levying on the caravans a departure duty, a travel duty, and an entry duty. The Tuareg carry on, furthermore, the trade in Negroes.

9 A verse admirably depicting the charms which the Arabs of the Sahara find in their nomadic life and the disdain which they profess for the Arabs of the Tell. [The Tell is a region in northeastern Algeria and northern Tunisia. It is a very fertile area and produces large grain crops. It attained great productivity under French rule. The Tell is the granary of the Sahara. The master of the Tell holds over the people of the Sahara the threat of famine. They are so conscious of this that they frankly acknowledge it in a phrase that has become a proverb: "We cannot be

Her head is ornamented with pure silk
From which escapes, in curling locks,
Her black hair perfumed with musk or
With the amber of Tunis.
Her teeth you would say were pearls
Set in the reddest of coral
And her eyes, veined with blood,
Wound like the arrows
Of the savage inhabitants of Bernou.[10]

Her saliva, I have tasted it.
It is the sugar of dried raisins
Or the honey of bees
When the springtime blossoms.
Her neck, it is the mast of a vessel
Which cleaves the deep seas
With its white sails
To drift according to the winds.

Her throat is like the peach
Seen ripening on a tree.
Her shoulders of polished ivory
And her rounded ribs
Are the proud sabers
Which the *djouad*
Draw on days wearied of gunpowder.
How many gallant horsemen
Have died for her on fighting!

O! How much I would like to possess
The best horse on earth
To ride alone and thoughtful
Close to her white she-camel!
That horse would be the torment of
The young men of the Sahara!

I hunt, I pray, I fast,
And follow the laws of the Prophet;
But, even if I were to go to Mecca,

Moslems, Jews, or Christians; we are forcibly the friends of our bellies."] [Translator's note]

    [10] A Negro kingdom in the south whose peoples still fight with poisoned arrows.

> I would never forget Meryem.
> Yes, Meryem
> With your black lashes
> You will always be beautiful,
> As pleasing as a gift.[11]

At the end of a few hours the heat makes itself felt; a halt (*meguil*) is made. The tents are pitched, breakfast is prepared, the horses are unbridled, allowed to graze. It is rest.

The sun goes lower, the heat lessens, it is two or three hours after midday. On your way, forward! You others, the bold horsemen, cause to be seen, in a brilliant *fantasia*,[12] what your horses are and what you are yourselves. The women are looking at you, show them what use you can make of a horse and rifle. Go on! More than one will be recompensed for his prowess. Do you see that Negro? He brings to one from among you the reward for your skill in handling a horse or in making use of a rifle; he is the messenger to whom one of the lovely spectators has entrusted her love. She has charged him with taking to the hero of the *fantasia* her ankle bracelets (*khrolkhral*) or her necklace of cloves (*mekhranga*).

But it is not enough to be a brave and skillful horseman. It is necessary to be prudent. You have a friend. Tomorrow you will give him your horse and your clothing, strongly recommending to him (your sister desires it)[13] that he show himself in the midst of the *goum* with your mount and clad like you, so that all the other horsemen will be deceived. You, you will go unnoticed, humble infantryman. You will march close to the she-camels bearing your new mistress. Be alert. Watch for a favorable moment and slip into the *aâtatouche*.[14] Go on!

---

11 "As pleasing as a gift": The Arab's saying that his mistress would always be as pleasing as a gift makes clear how much his people are still subject to the allure and corruption of gifts.

12 *Fantasia:* a dashing display of horsemanship and prowess with weapons. [Translator's note]

13 "Your sister desires it": sister, in this instance, means mistress.

14 ". . . of the two *takhts er-Rúm* or camel coaches, in the equipage of the Persian aga, which are borne in such sort that each is suspended by the four shafts, between the withers of a fore and the shoulders of an after camel. By every shaft there goes a lad, and in the midst a lad, upon both sides, six for a *takht*. Where the wild road is unequal, with the strength of their arms, they rule the sway of this high uneasy carriage. The *takhts* are gallantly painted and adorned, there is

She is as impatient as you. She extends her hand; profit from that aid and make your movements swifter than suspicion.

In love, as in war, fortune is for the daring, but dangers are for them also. If these rendezvous are frequent and almost always succeed, life is at stake. Lovers thus surprised would both be sure to perish.

But who would betray them? All those about them are for them. The lover apprises his friends of his good fortune. All have wanted to help his happiness and ten or twelve *douros* have been sent to his mistress. That is still not all. Her emissary has received two or three *douros* and lastly, money has been distributed to the slaves and to the servants of her tent. Thus all those servitors keep good watch and they warn the lover of the instant he should emerge from the *aâtatouche* when, at the approach of nightfall, the setting up of the camp spreads disorder and confusion everywhere.

Before the setting of the sun the chieftains have found a site suitable for the night's camp. Water, grass, and the bushes which serve to make fires (*el guetof, el oueera,* and *el chiehh*) should be found there. Upon arrival at the designated spot each man pitches, or causes to be pitched, his tent. The horses are unbridled and they are hobbled like the camels. The Negroes go in search of grass and wood, the women prepare the food, everyone sups. A thousand scenes give to the embodiment of the camp an aspect filled with charm and originality; then complete darkness envelops it, unless there is moonlight. The fires are extinguished, no light glows in the shadows. In the Sahara it is not known what oil and wax are.[15] Immediately after supper each

room in them that a man may lie at his length or sit up . . . . Upon the bearing harness of the *takht* camels are shields of scarlet, full of mirrors, with crests of ostrich plumes, and beset with ranks of little bells, which at each slow camel's foot-fall jingle . . . The hind camel paces very unhandsomely, for that he may not put his muzzle through the glass panel, his head and huge long neck is drawn down under the floorboard of his unwieldy burden, which is under the height of his shoulders, with much distress of the weary beast in the long marches. Not a little stately are those camel litters, with the ladders and gay trappings, marching in the empty way of the desert;—they remain perchance of the old Byzantine pageantry" (Charles M. Doughty, *Travels in Arabia Deserta,* Vol. 1, p. 105). This translator is of the opinion that the *aâtatouche* of General Daumas is an Algerian version of Doughty's *takhts er-Rúm*. [Translator's note]

[15] Since their frequent relations with us, the desert chieftains have used with pleasure the candles they buy from us on the coast.

tent designates a man to keep watch over the baggage and animals. He is charged with preventing the thefts which even his active vigilance can scarcely prevent.

Thieves are not the only ones to wait for nightfall. Also at that hour, and protected by the darkness, the lover, advised by his mistress, stealthily approaches the tent where she is lying, lifts the edge, guided by a devoted slave, and takes the place of the husband who, wearied from the day's travel, is sleeping in the room for the men (*khralfa mtâa redjal*). For in the desert tents always have two distinct chambers, one for the men, the other for the women. Furthermore, a man cannot, without shame, spend the entire night with his wife. Nothing therefore hinders amorous interviews. It is not the presence of one or more of the three other wives, whom the law permits to Moslems, that is an obstacle; it is necessary to believe in the Arab proverb: "Only the Jewess surpasses *Chitann* (Satan) in malice, but close after Satan comes the Moslem woman." It is unheard of in the desert that the women betray each other.

At times, however, the adventure is too dangerous. The woman then leaves the tent when everyone is asleep and reaches a place which she has designated to her lover in advance, through one of the obligatory intermediaries, a Negro or a drover.

It is also at the hour when happy lovers meet that vengeful projects are carried out. A repudiated lover penetrates into the tent of her who has spurned him, approaches, and kills her with a shot from a pistol. At the sound of the detonation all rise, all run about, there is much shouting, but the murderer has had time to disappear and almost always the crime, committed without witnesses, goes unpunished.

All these adventures are frequent in the Sahara—willingly or unwillingly an Arab woman always has lovers. The jealousy and precautions of the husbands overexcite and impel to excess upon restraining the licentiousness of the women. Whatever their class, the women spend their lives inventing ruses to deceive their husbands when young and helping the amours of others when old.[16] All intrigues are woven by the intervention of go-betweens (*âdjouza*). It is they whose gilded tongues and diabolical machinations dispose the young women to yield

16 There are, however, honorable exceptions.

and who supervise the rendezvous. They take advantage of all methods to insinuate themselves and are successful, above all, when they attack on the weak side, that is, the love of gifts.

Night has passed, the sky becomes gilded. It is the moment for departure, the second day's march is to begin. At that moment the chieftains send out *chouafin* (scouts), charged with reconnoitering the enemy's position and of judging by outward appearances the state of his morale and the number of reinforcements he has received. These scouts advance with caution and travel only at night when they draw near the enemy's camp. Then a man on foot disengages himself and, taking advantage of all the broken terrain to avoid being seen, often clothed in rags, boldly penetrates at night into the midst of the *douars*. He assures himself of the number of infantrymen, of horses, of tents. He observes if there is laughter, if there is entertainment, or whether sorrow prevails in the camp, and then returns to make a report on his observations.

The *chouafin*, in a body, wait for daybreak in a hidden spot, impatient to see what the enemy's attitude will be at sunrise. If the *fantasia* is performed, if rifles are fired, if cries of joy, songs, and the notes of the flute are heard, it is certain that he has received reinforcements and is not uneasy about the coming attack. The assailing tribe continues on its way just until it is no more than nine or ten leagues from the enemy. It has advanced but by short stages; the baggage, the women, the infantrymen are, moreover, cause for slowness. But holding it back, above all, are the orders of the chieftains who wish to give time to reflect to those whom they are going to attack.

It is prudent so to act and powerful motives determine the chieftains to do so. Who knows? Perhaps they will receive proposals for peace with many gifts for them, the preponderant personages in the councils? Are examples lacking? Is it not the custom? For them the cottonstuffs, the woolen garments (*kate*), the silver-mounted rifles, the ankle bracelets (*khrolkhral*) and, lastly, the *douros*! Then, it must be said, when the affair takes that turn it is very close to being settled amicably.

The two opposing sides are separated by a distance of but ten leagues, and no proposal, direct or indirect, has been exchanged. Does the tribe recognize itself as incapable to resist, or will it accept the struggle? If the tribe eschews combat, its most influential Marabouts are gathered, furnished with money and gifts to which each has contributed his share. The holy men arrive at the enemy's camp in the middle of the night, under the protection of a chieftain warned in advance and swiftly swayed by numerous gifts. He conducts the emissaries to another chieftain, who also permits himself to accept the gifts which are proffered him, and both accompany the messengers of peace to a third personage, and so on, until all those whose say-so is powerful have been won over. Only then [do] the Marabouts, sure of the good will of those who listen to them, formulate the proposals they were charged to make and express themselves thus: "We have come but for the love of God. You know that we are Marabouts and that we desire only good. It is necessary, in our opinion, that you arrange matters with the Moslems who sent us. That would be worth more than drawing down upon ourselves all the misfortunes of war, ruin, death. If you desire good, God will bless you, you, your wives, your children, your mares, your she-camels. If you desire evil, may it fall on you. We repeat, make peace and may God curse the devil!"

After some difficulties arising from [a matter of] form, the chieftains end by replying to the Marabouts: "All right! We will make peace because of God and because of you, but under the following conditions:

1. You shall return to us the objects, the goods or the animals which were carried off when your people pillaged our caravan at such and such a place.
2. You shall pay the *dya* (blood price)[17] for our people whom you killed on such and such a day.
3. You shall also return to us all that which was taken from us in the way of livestock on such and such a day by your people in such and such a *khrotefa*.
4. You shall also restore to us all the camels and horses which your thieves stole from us and which are still among you."

---

17 The *dya* in the Sahara is paid with fifty *hachy* or three-year-old camels or, furthermore, three hundred sheep. One *hachy*, then, is worth only six sheep.

The Marabouts accept these conditions, upon making themselves guarantors. Then the Holy Book of Sidi-Abd-Allah is brought and all the chieftains vow to make peace. The oath sworn, those who had come so that blood would not be spilled return to their tribe to inform it of what has been decided and to force it to carry out the conditions for which they have made themselves guarantors.

On the following day the tribe which has accorded peace continues on its way and sets up its camp one league at the most from the enemy. Scarcely has it been set up when the Marabouts and all the chieftains of the opposing party arrive to bring the agreed ransom. The leaders of the two rival camps join and again swear on the Book of Sidi-Abd-Allah: "By the truth of Sidi-Abd-Allah we swear that there shall no longer be between us *razzias*, or thefts, or murders, or *ousiga* (reprisals); that we are brothers and that our rifles shall never be fired but in unison."

The Marabouts of both sides then read the *fatahh*[18] and conclude by saying: "May God bless you, our children, for having thus buried the knife of evil (*khrodmi cheurr*) and may He cause you to prosper with your families and your goods."

These Marabouts are then visited by the chieftains of one side and of the other, who give them offerings called *zyara* (visit).

Peace concluded, the tribe which had set itself in movement retraces its steps and makes of its departure one of the noisiest of *fantasias*. The horses caracole, rifles reverberate, women shriek; it is joy, good fortune, delirium. Some dozen of the chieftains of that tribe remain in the midst of their enemies of the day before and receive from them a sumptuous hospitality and even rich gifts. Then, at their departure, they bring along with them, in turn, some of the chieftains [who had been] their hosts and accord to these new allies their generous acceptance [of them].

These truces last for quite some time; that is to say, one or two years. To be sure, peace would not have been concluded if the Marabouts who arrived to solicit it had not presented themselves in the middle of the night. If they had arrived in full daylight, the Arabs,

---

[18] The *fatahh*: religious invocation.

witnesses of their intrigues, would have cried out, out of jealousy:[19]
"By the sin of our wives we will fight. So-and-so has received a woolen
garment, So-and-so some money, someone else jewels, this one cottonstuffs, that one arms, and we, whose brothers are dead, we, whose
herds have been carried off, we have not received anything; yes! We
swear it by Sidi-Abd-Allah, gunpowder shall speak!"

Often the gunpowder speaks without the envious having had to
complain of the gifts made to the chieftains, without their having
prevented the latter from debating and accepting conditions from
which they extract no profit. It is when the tribe has resolved to resist
that it prepares for combat. It allows the enemy to approach within
one day's march; no advances, no proposals. The enemy continues on
his way the following day and makes camp two leagues, at the most,
from those who are waiting for the attack.

The scouts of both sides meet, mutually taunt each other, and pre-
lude the hostilities by insults. They are the *mecherahbin* (provocateurs); they exchange a few random shots and exclaim:

(One side): O Fatma! Daughters of Fatma! Night has fallen, why
continue today? Tomorrow shall be called your day.
(The other side): Dogs, sons of dogs, until tomorrow! If you are men
you will confront us!

The scouts withdraw, the chieftains of each side organize with all
speed a guard of one hundred horsemen and one hundred infantrymen
for the safety of the respective camps. The following day careful observation is made. If one of the two sides strikes its tents, the other
does also; but if, leaving its tents pitched, it advances for combat with
its cavalry, infantry, and women riding camels, its example is followed.

The horsemen of the two tribes confront each other. The women
are in the rear, ready to inflame the combatants by their shrieks and
applause. They are protected by the infantry which, at the same time,
forms the reserve. Battle is joined by small bodies of ten to fifteen

19 "Out of jealousy": This passage in my work again gives a facet of Arab life.
It proves, too, how much need the chieftains have of ability, prudence, and policy
to lead a people of whom the least shepherd wants to know about the affairs of his
country.

horsemen who bear down on the flanks and try to turn back the enemy.[20]

The chieftains, at the head of a quite compact body, keep to the center. Soon the scene becomes lively and more heated. The young horsemen, the bravest and the best mounted, hurl themselves forward, carried away by ardor and the thirst for blood. They bare their heads, chant war songs, and arouse themselves to combat with these yells: "Where are they, those who have mistresses? It is in front of their eyes that the warriors fight today! . . . Where are they, those who close to the chieftains are forever speaking of their courage? It is to-day that the tongue should be long and not in idle talks. . . . Where are they, those who run after a reputation? . . . Forward, sons of gun-powder! You see those sons of Jews before you. Our sabers should be watered with their blood. Their goods, we'll give them to our women. . . . Fly, young men, fly! Balls do not slay. It is only Destiny that kills."

Such yells inflame the horsemen. They make their horses rear and their rifles leap. All expressions demand blood, there is a melee and it ends in a hand-to-hand saber clash.

However, one side withdraws and begins to fall back on the camels

---

[20] "Upon departing from the tribe of the Beni-Selyman I was accompanied as far as Mosul by four sheiks (*chikh*) and five or six hundred horsemen. I had re-mained under their tents for a long time; I had bought many mares or colts from them; they knew me, we were on the best of terms. One day the conversation touched upon the subject of their interminable wars with the Turks and I expressed a desire to learn their way of fighting. With a great deal of good nature and gaiety they consented to perform in front of me a representation of their attacks. Here is how they proceed. The Arabs wheel continually in front of the Turkish horsemen, the latter ever advancing and the Arabs ever yielding ground, out of rifle range, only to return; thus having no other goal than that of tiring the enemy's horses and of doing him, if a favorable opportunity presents itself, a great deal of harm with impunity. But, should reinforcements arrive, above all of cannon, or should they find themselves hemmed in in a bad position, it is then that an Arab might address his mare thus:

" 'Amouna, thou knowest that thou wert foaled under my tent, that I have often slept on thy shoulder, that, with respect to milk and dates, thou hast always come before my own children and that, when I have come across water, it is yet thou who hast always drunk first.

" 'Well now, today my life is in thy spirit and legs. Wilt thou allow me to be captured by these dogs and wilt thou consent, for the rest of thy days, to being tied up in a stable where thou canst not breathe the free, pure air of the desert? No! That would be a dishonor for thy noble family. Save, then, him who has so tenderly looked after thee.' " (*Travel in Upper Asia,* by M. Pétiniaud, Inspector-General of Studs.)

carrying the women. Then the women of both sides can be heard shrieking. Some utter cries of joy to animate the victors further, the others utter cries of rage and bloody imprecations to rally the shaken courage of their husbands or of their brothers: "Look at them now! Those famous warriors who use white [silver] stirrups and splendid garments at feasts and weddings! Look at them now! Fleeing and even abandoning their women! O Jews! Sons of Jews! Dismount! We'll ride your horses and, from today onward, you will no longer be numbered among men. Oh, the cowards! May God curse them!"

In the face of such insults ardor revives among the vanquished. They make a vigorous effort. Supported by the fire of the infantrymen who are in reserve they regain ground and throw the enemy back as far as the midst of his women who, in their turn, curse those whom they applauded a moment before.

Combat resumes on the ground which separates the women of the two tribes. The struggle in its changing fortunes has been very heated and soon the side which has had the most men and horses wounded, which has lost the greater number of men and, above all, which has seen its most valiant chieftains fall, takes flight, despite the exhortations and the prayers of some forceful men who, desirous of rallying the others, look from right to left, seeking to regain the victory. They yell: "Are there men here or are there not? Maintain your spirit! If you flee, your women will be carried off and only shame will be left to you. Die! It cannot then be said: 'They have fled!' Die! You shall yet live!"

Then there takes place a truly touching and beautiful scene. The highest-ranking chieftain, in despair at being vanquished, hurls himself into the melee, seeking death. But he is restrained by the young men, who surround him and beg him to withdraw.

"You are our father," they say. "What would become of us should we lose you? It is for us to die for you. We do not wish to remain like a flock without a shepherd."

Some warriors still want to make a stand, but the general rout drags them along. Soon they are close to their women. Then each one, seeing that all is lost, tries to save what is dearest to him. As much ground to the rear as possible is covered. Now and again they halt.

A stand is made to confront the enemy should he be in pursuit.

A foolhardy desperation has sometimes changed the aspect of the matter. Aïssa-ben-el-Chérif, a boy of fourteen, was mounted on horseback with his tribe to repulse an attack led by Sy-el-Djedid. When the men of the Arbâa gave ground and took flight, the boy, dashing in front of them, tried to make them halt.

"What then! You are men and you are afraid! You have been reared in the midst of gunpowder and you do not know how to touch it off! Have you taken such good care of your mares only to make use of them for flight?"

"Djedid! Djedid!" yelled the others. "Behold Djedid!"

"Djedid!" retorted the boy. "It is one man alone who makes you flee! See then that terrible warrior who has put hundreds of men to flight and whom a boy halts in his victory!"

Aïssa clapped spurs to his horse. He reached the redoubtable warrior. Djedid was not on guard; what did he have to fear from a boy? But the boy threw himself on the warrior's neck, clasped him, and, leaving his saddle, clung to him with one hand while with the other he sought to stab him with his knife. Djedid, astounded by such audacity, and hampered in his movements, tried in vain to free himself, but he was not calm enough to parry the blows the boy was giving him. At last he had no others means of escape but to allow himself to fall from his horse, hoping to crush Aïssa in his fall; but the boy evaded him and, springing on the redoubtable chieftain's horse, he rejoined his tribe, where he showed off a trophy which caused the oldest horsemen to redden at that moment of panic which a boy had resisted.

The victor, if he does not make a bridge of gold to the vanquished, can ruin him completely. But the thirst for pillage carries him away. The men disband and dream only of booty. Someone rifles an infantryman, another a fallen horseman, this one leads off a horse, that one a Negro. Thanks to the disorder, the boldest men of the [vanquished] tribe are yet able to save their wives and sometimes their tents.

After the pillaging the horsemen of the victorious tribe dream of going to rest [but] the chieftains restrain them: "We have done much killing, we have carried off horses, captured women, taken rifles; we have refreshed our hearts while making orphans of these sons of dogs. The best thing to do is to go to sleep this evening at such and such a place, for our enemies, supported by reinforcements, might very well attack us tonight."

All the baggage [camels] are made to travel in the van, a strong reserve forms the rearguard and protects it. On the first day and the following travel is performed until nightfall.

In that kind of warfare the greatest respect is observed toward the female captives. Men of low birth despoil them of their jewels, but the chieftains hold it a point of honor to send them back to their husbands with their camels, their jewels, and their clothes. They even hasten to clothe, in order to restore, those who have been despoiled.

In the desert prisoners are not taken, heads are not cut off, and there is a horror of mutilating the wounded. After the combat the latter are left to extricate themselves from their straits as best they can. No further attention is paid to them. There are some rare examples of cruelty. Those are the vengeance of men who have recognized in the enemy *goum* the murderers of some person whom they held dear, of a brother, of a friend.

Upon returning to its lands the tribe is received by an unrivaled fête. General rejoicing is portrayed by the liveliest of demonstrations. The women align their camels in one rank and utter cries of joy at regular intervals. The young men execute an unbridled *fantasia* before their eyes. There are greetings, embraces, questions. Food is prepared for one's own and for one's allies. The chieftains gather the sum to be distributed to the latter. A simple horseman never receives less than ten *douros* or some object of that value. That compensation is called *zebeun*; it is obligatory and given over and above the booty which each might have been able to gather. There are even added, for the rider who lost a horse, three camels or one hundred *douros*.

It goes without saying that more than ten *douros* are given to the chieftains of the allied tribes; the chieftains whose influence has been decisive. They receive their share like the others, but they secretly receive money or gifts of a certain value (rugs, tents, arms, horses), besides.

The allies are given a generous hospitality and the following day when they depart for their territories the chieftains mount their horses and accompany them. After they have traveled together for two or three hours the oath is mutually renewed, that of never uttering but one sole yell, of being but one and the same rifle, of coming in the morning if one is summoned in the morning, and of coming at night if one is summoned at night.[21]

It is natural to seek to learn why the tribe—which is going to be attacked and which does not want to make the sacrifices necessary to procure peace—why does it, a nomadic tribe, not take flight instead of waiting for an onslaught?

To flee: that would be to ask to be pursued and attacked in the disorder of a retreat; that would be to draw far away from one's lands, to risk lack of water for the herds; even perhaps to encounter another enemy who would most assuredly seize such an occasion for pillage and vengeance.

The wisest course is to choose one's ground, gather one's allies, and await the enemy, if one considers oneself to be the stronger, or to make concessions, if one feels oneself to be the weaker.

"O my God! Save us and save our horses. Every day we lie down in a new land. Perhaps He remembers our evenings with the flutes and drums."

OBSERVATIONS OF THE EMIR ABD-EL-KADER

How can foreign peoples struggle against us, we who have raised ourselves to the highest point of honor and even above all the tribes gathered at the great assemblies? Do we not take against the enemy our horses of a pure breed who, terrible as furious lions, can gallop headlong on the dangerous mountain paths?

---

[21] In the desert, if hatreds are hereditary and lively, in return warm friendships are as numerous as they are profound. Here are some verses which prove to what degree of delicacy and devotion friendship among the Arabs can be carried: "If a friend does not go blindly like the child, if he does not expose himself voluntarily to Death, on forgetting that suicide is a crime, he shall not have a place in the tents of our tribes.

"I will obey the summons of my friend when the morning light shall be the reflection from swords, when the shades of night shall be the shadow of the dust raised by horses' hooves. I will go to die or to be happy. The least of the sacrifices to which I have agreed is that of dying. Can I live far from the haven I love? Can I bear the absence of neighbors to whom I am accustomed?"

I have prepared, in case Fortune is unfaithful to me, a noble courser of perfect form which none other can rival in speed.

I also have a gleaming saber which cuts through the bodies of my enemies in a single slash.

And yet, Fortune has treated me as if I had never had the pleasure of mounting a drinker of the wind; as if I had never rested my heart on the virginal bosom of a beloved woman with limbs adorned with gold bracelets; as if I had never felt the sorrows of separation; as if I had never been present at the moving spectacle of our purebred horses surprising the enemy at break of day; as if, lastly, after a defeat I had never rallied fugitives to combat upon shouting at them:

> Fatma, daughters of Fatma!
> Death is a toll levied on our heads.
> Turn your horses' heads and renew the charge!
> Time turns back on itself and returns.
> Ah! Would that I could throw the world on its face!

6

CUSTOMS OF WAR

My horse is worth more than anything else:
More than my father, more than my uncles.
More than the goods of this earth.
No sultan has mounted his equal.
He is a Marabout; the women come to visit him.

When, after a *razzia* or an expedition, the Arabs of the desert return to their *douars*, they undertake the sharing of the booty. That sharing is done in equal parts. However, some preassessments are exercised in special cases.

Thus the horseman who has killed another in war has the right to the dead man's horse, arms, clothing, tack, knapsack, and saddlebags. *In effect, he has risked his life to gain a life; he must answer in the presence of God for a death he has caused, rightly or wrongly.* A captured horse, whose master has not been killed, is comprised in the booty to be shared.

If a horseman has been killed by many individuals who fired together, without its being possible to determine by whose hand he died, the booty is shared equally; in other localities the booty reverts to the chieftain when it has not been possible to single out the rifle that killed.

A horseman learning only after the combat that he has killed an enemy and causing the fact to be corroborated by witnesses obtains the restitution of all the booty of the dead man.

When one tribe goes on an expedition against another tribe, each individual keeps the loot he has been able to take in the way of *haïks,* burnooses, arms, and garments, but everything in the way of tents, herds, horses, mules, camels, goods, and grain is shared exactly. Only the chieftain has a right, over and above [his share], to thirty or forty ewes or three or four she-camels, according to circumstances. If he did not take part in person he will still be given a share which is called "the knot of the sheik" (*aâkeud echikh*).

If some individual, not wishing to form part of the expedition, has lent his mare to a friend, he shares the booty which the latter has been able to reap. If the animal perishes and a capture has been made, pre-assessment is made and the owner is reimbursed for the price of the mare. The animal had marched in the interests of the tribe; if there has been no success, and the animal perishes, the owner bears the loss; *he asked for his fortune.* He who has offered provisions to a party of horsemen has a right to a share *mezrag* (lance) if the party is successful; he interested himself in the expedition.

A lance [is given] to the farrier of the tribe; he has contributed by his labor and his skill to the success of the enterprise. To kill him is an infamous act; it would fall upon the children of the guilty tribe and anathema would follow them everywhere. He should also be spared who, after having removed his burnoose, goes to the enemy, the butt of his rifle in the air. The shepherds also have their lives spared.

A special share is always given to those who were sent out as scouts before falling upon the enemy. It is just recompense for these *chouafin* (scouts) who offer the sacrifice of their lives for the triumph of their people. If a *chouaf* has lost his mare, she is replaced with one hundred Spanish *douros.* That is not an exaggerated price, for [only] the best-mounted horsemen are chosen as scouts.

A party which returns with booty accords a lance to the woman of distinction who emerges from her tent to utter joyous cries in its honor.

In an affair of *nif* (amour propre) the lovely women who were taken along to animate the combatants have a right to a part of the prize.

He who has lent his rifle takes a quarter of the share which falls to the borrower.

An Arab finds a horse at pasture, far from the eyes of its owner. His tribe has been attacked or is ready to leave on an expedition; he takes the horse, puts a borrowed saddle on its back. That saddle is not complete; he finds stirrups to the right, a girth to the left, a bridle and breastplate somewhere else. Finally he is equipped; he departs and returns with booty. The owner of the horse has no right to [a share of] it. Had his horse been killed, he would have been reimbursed (in case of success), but if the horse is returned safe and sound he has no claim to make. *The horse was naught but the instrument of God to render service to a brave horseman who risked himself in the general interest.*

The owners of the accessories of the saddle have a right to a certain share of the prize. The nomads of the desert have, in a fable wholly to [the liking of] Arab taste, specified the respective rights of each owner.

The saddletree says to the horseman: "Are you thinking of keeping the booty all to yourself? Who furnished you with a seat? And what would you have done if you had not found me there?"

"Fine thing!" exclaims the girth instantly. "That service you're boasting about, is it then so great? You would have been more hindrance than you would have been assistance if I had not held you on the horse's back."

"Softly, softly," speak the stirrups then. "Both of you would have been useful, I agree. But, I pray you, tell me who supported the rider when he failed to throw himself forward? And on what was he resting when he had to make use of his weapon to fell the enemy from whom he took the booty which you are disputing so hotly? Who permitted him to see far ahead, to dismount and remount, be it to strike, be it to escape the blows which threatened him?"

"It was you," replies the bridle. "No one can escape the truth, and yet, nevertheless, my children, by God, Master of the world, our horseman would have been much less well off than he is today if he had nothing but your assistance. You would scarcely have taken the road to the booty and you would still have been far away, if I had not led you there. Then stop these arguments! The palm [laurel] belongs to me, for only I was able to make you reach the goal."

"Ah! That's a little too much!" The horse—who up until that point had been listening without saying a word—snorted ironically. "I don't know why I had thought that the biggest share was mine. I thought that I saw you lying forgotten in a corner and I thought to myself that you would not have been gathered together but for the fact that someone found me. I was undoubtedly dreaming. It was you who brought me here. I acknowledge that I was mistaken. Take me back then, as soon as possible, to my pasture, where, at least, I shall no longer have to listen to your intrigues."

To put a stop to all those arguments the horseman divides his booty into six equal shares, giving one to the saddletree, one to the girth, one to the bridle, keeping the other three for himself. He returns the horse to its pasture upon saying to it: "*I shall not give thee anything, but with thee rests the honor of having been useful to thy tribe.*"

He who lends a complete saddle has a right to half of a share of the prize. That sharing is called the *âadet esserdj* (custom of the saddle).

Before departing on an expedition the *goum* makes the following invocation:

O Sidi Abd-el-Kader-el-Djelali
O Sidi Chikh-ben-ed-Dine
O Sidi el-Hadj-bou-Hafeus
If we are successful and if we return safe and sound
We promise to each of you a camel.
Protect us!

These three camels are always designated by the Marabouts before any repartition. The repartition is not made, as can well be imagined, without numerous disputes. To forestall or suppress them the *meka-dinn* have been instituted. Sometimes the chieftains choose five or six

individuals reputed as being sage. Sometimes after a *razzia* or a capture, the booty is divided into four equal parts. Those who have carried out the undertaking are divided into four factions and each faction
nominates a *mekadem* charged with carrying out the subdivision. The
mekadinn search for and bring about the restitution of all objects
which might have been hidden by people of bad faith; women's
jewelry, or money, or coral.

When an Arab is suspected of a wrongdoing of that nature and the
object of the fraud cannot be found in his possession, the *mekadinn*
make him swear by Sidi-ben-Abd-Allah and that oath absolves him.
In the Sahara Sidi-ben-Abd-Allah is held in great veneration; no one
would dare to invoke his name by swearing falsely, under penalty of
death or of seeing his herds waste away.

The *mekadinn* are recognized as honest men among rogues. They
are well treated and receive good remuneration, which often consists
of the objects left over after the repartition.

> My horse is worth more than anything else:
> More than my father, more than my uncles.
> More than the goods of this earth.
> No sultan has mounted his equal.
> He is a Marabout; the women come to visit him.

Observations of the Emir Abd-el-Kader

I have surprised them with purebred horses with sleek coats, their
foreheads adorned with stars heralding good fortune, their flanks made
slender by gallops, with firm hard flesh, by falling on them like the
cloud charged with lightning which covers a gorge.

It is a horse which, without ever tiring itself, always ends by making
its rider beg for mercy. Its head is lean, its ears and lips fine, its
nostrils wide, its neck light, its skin black and soft, its coat sleek, and its
joints wide. *By the Head of the Prophet!* It is of a noble breed and you
would never ask how much it had cost if you had seen it go to meet
the enemy!

When you see the horses of the *goum* going proudly, heads high
and making the air reverberate with their neighing, rest assured that

victory travels with them. But when, on the contrary, you see the horses of the *goum* going dispiritedly, heads hanging, without neighing and switching their tails, believe that Fortune has abandoned them.

However, Almighty God is wiser than anyone!

Oh, I wish to see my blood flow over my *haïk* [which is as] white as the ivory of the Sudan. It would only be the more beautiful for it.

7

THE CHASE OF THE OSTRICH

The man who devotes himself to the chase
makes daily progress in courage. He learns
a contempt for accidents.

In the desert there are two chief means of hunting the ostrich: on
horseback; from blinds; and, lastly, a third, which is nothing but a
variety of the second. This consists of killing the animal when it comes
to quench its thirst at a spring.

The true chase is that on horseback. It is, as compared to killing
from the blind, that which is, among us [the French], the hunting of
the stag; a pleasure of the gentleman, of the king, we used to say; and
not the career of a whipper-in and man on foot. It is not enough to
kill, an effort is made.[1]

The general training given to the horse is not sufficient. For that
particular type of chase a special preparation is necessary, as, for our
racehorse, training is necessary for a few days immediately preceding
the contest.

Here is the training method customarily used for the horses of the
Sahara: Seven to eight days before the hunt, hay or grass is eliminated
and only barley is fed. The horses are watered only once a day, at the

---

[1] The Arabs of the Sahara love hunting passionately and their religion permits
them to hunt game whose flesh is not forbidden. It is also permitted to hunt those
animals whose flesh is forbidden, if, like the jackal and the wild boar, they cause
damage.

setting of the sun, an hour at which the water begins to cool and they are bathed. They are taken on a long daily ride, alternately walking and galloping, during which one makes sure that nothing is missing from the accouterments appropriate for the chase of the ostrich and of which I am going to speak [later on]. After those seven or eight days, says the Arab, the horse's belly disappears, while his neck, breast, and croup are in hard flesh. Then the animal is ready to withstand fatigue. That training of the horse is called *techaha*.

The accouterments are also modified with a view to lightening them. The stirrups used are much less heavy than usual, the saddletree very light, the two *kerbouss* (pommel and cantle) diminished in height, and the *stara* (saddlecover) is removed. The breastplate is also removed and out of seven saddleblankets only two remain.

The bridle also undergoes numerous metamorphoses. The blinders and the cheekpieces are removed as being too heavy. The bit is then simply fastened to a sufficiently stout camelhide thong, without a throatlatch, held in place by a species of brow-band, also a thong; the reins should be light, but very strong.

The horses are shod all around.

The most favorable season for that chase is during the great heat of summer. The higher the temperature has risen, the less vigor the ostrich has to defend itself. The Arabs pinpoint that moment by saying that it is that time when a man, standing up, does not cast a shadow longer than a shoe-sole.

[That chase] is a veritable expedition which lasts for seven to eight days. It demands preparatory measures, which are concerted by some ten horsemen united in *akeud*, as for a *razzia*.

Each horseman is accompanied by one of his servants, then referred to as the *zemmal* (hunt servant) and mounted on a camel bearing four goatskins filled with water, barley for the horse, wheat flour (*deguig*), another species of grilled flour (*rouina*), dates, a pot (*mordjem*) for cooking, long narrow cords, a sewing-needle, horseshoes, and spare nails.

The horseman should wear only a chemise of wool or cotton and woolen drawers. He covers his head and ears with a piece of light material, called *haouly* in the desert, [which is] held in place by camelhide thong. On his feet are slippers held in place by thongs; he wears light leggings (*trabag*). He does not carry a rifle or pistol or gunpowder; his only weapon is a club of wild olive or tamarind, four or five feet long, with a very heavy tip.

A start on a hunt is not made until after the hunters have been apprised by travelers, or caravans, or scouts sent for the purpose, of a large number of ostriches at a given spot. Ordinarily the ostriches are found in the places where there is a great deal of pasturage and where it has rained very shortly before. According to the Arabs, as soon as the ostrich sees the lightning flash and a storm brewing, no matter where, it runs toward the spot, even if it is at a great distance. Ten days' travel are nothing to an ostrich. In the desert it is said of a man skilled in looking after flocks and finding the things necessary to them: "He is like the ostrich. He goes where he sees the lightning flash."

A start is made in the morning. After one or two days' travel, upon arriving close to the place where the ostriches have been pointed out and when their traces begin to be seen, a halt is made and camp set up.

On the following day two quick-witted servants, completely nude and having but a handkerchief in the way of a loincloth, are sent on reconnaissance. Each carries a goatskin of water (*chibouta*) hung from the waist and a little bread. They continue onward just until they encounter the ostriches, which always place themselves, say the Arabs, on high ground. Just as soon as the scouts have seen them, they lie down and watch. Then one of them stays behind and the other returns to alert the *goum*. He has seen sometimes thirty, forty, or sixty ostriches, for there exist, it is asserted, flocks (*djeliba*) of that number. At other times, above all in the mating season, ostriches are found but in three or four couples.

The horsemen, guided by the servant who came to apprise them, travel quietly to where the ostriches are. The closer they draw to the hill where the ostriches have been pointed out, the more precautions they take in order not to be seen. Finally, having arrived at the last bit of terrain which can conceal them, they dismount. Two scouts crawl ahead to assure themselves afresh that the ostriches are still in the same place. If the first sightings are confirmed, each man waters his horse, but moderately, from the water carried on the camels, for it is very rare to come upon a spot where there are springs. All the baggage is deposited in the same spot where the halt is made, without leaving a watchman, there is such certainty of finding the site again. Each horseman carries at his side a *chibouta*. The servants and the camels follow the horses' tracks. Each camel carries no more than the horse's barley supper, its own supper, and water for the men and animals.

The position of the ostriches being well known, council is held, the ten horsemen divide and form a circle within which they surround the game at a very great distance so as not to be glimpsed, for the ostrich has excellent eyesight. The servants wait at the place where the horsemen divided. Then as soon as they see each man in place, they go straight toward the ostriches. The ostriches flee, terrified, but encounter the horsemen, who at first do nothing but try to make them reenter the circle. The ostriches thus begin to exhaust their strength on a swift run, for, as soon as surprised, "*they do not regulate their pace.*" They repeatedly renew that run, always trying to break out of the circle and always reentering, frightened by the horsemen. At the first signs of fatigue, the hunters gallop toward them. At the end of a certain length of time the flock disperses, the weakened ostriches are seen to spread their wings. That is an indication of great weariness. The horsemen, from that moment sure of their quarry, rein back their horses.

Each hunter selects an ostrich, goes after it, overtakes it, and, be it from behind, be it from the side, deals it a tremendous rap on the head with the club of which I have spoken. The head is bald and very sensitive, the other parts of the body offer more resistance. The ostrich, rudely struck, falls, and the horseman hastens to dismount to bleed it, being careful to hold the neck away from the body so that the blood will not stain the wings. The male ostrich when it is bled, particularly in front of its little ones, utters deplorable moans. The female does not utter a sound of any kind.

When the ostrich is on the point of being overtaken by the horseman it is so weary that, should the hunter not wish to kill it, it is easy for him to herd it quietly along, guiding it with his club. The ostrich can scarcely walk.

Immediately after having bled the ostrich it is carefully skinned so as not to spoil the plumes, then the skin is spread on a tree or on a horse. The camels come up and the inside of the remains is liberally sprinkled with salt. The servants light fires, put on the cooking-pots and boil on high heat all the fat from the animal for a long time. When it has become very liquid it is poured into a sort of pouch made out of the skin from the haunch to the foot, solidly attached to its lower part; in another place, the fat would spoil. The fat from an ostrich in good condition should fill both its legs.

When the ostrich broods it is very thin and then its fat will far from fill its two legs. At that time it is not hunted but for the value of its plumage.

The rest of the flesh is used for the hunters' supper. They eat it seasoned with pepper and flour.

The servants have watered the horses and have given them their barley. Everyone is somewhat refreshed and haste is made, no matter what the fatigue of the chase, to return to the spot where the baggage was left. There a halt of forty-eight hours is made, to rest the horses. During that time they are the objects of the greatest of care; then a return is made to the tents. Sometimes the fruits of the hunt are sent back to the *douar*, the servants return with provisions, and, based upon new observations, the enterprise is repeated.

In the desert the male ostrich is called *délim*, the female *reumda*, the young a year old *ral*, over a year old *ouled gleub*, over two years old *ouled bou gleubtin*. Finally, in its third year, the ostrich is designated under the name of *garah*. After that period the ostrich has attained its full development.

Uses of the Fat and of the Remains of the Ostrich

Ostrich fat is used to prepare food, *couscous*, for example. It is also eaten with bread. The Arabs make use of it, furthermore, as a remedy in a large number of maladies. For fever, with that fat and the doughy part of bread, a kind of pâté is made. It is given to an invalid to eat, who should not drink during the day. For kidney ailments and rheumatic pains, the afflicted parts are rubbed just until the fat has penetrated. Then the invalid lies down on the burning sand, his head carefully covered. Heavy sweating takes place and the cure is complete. For liver ailments, the fat, lightly heated and become like oil, then lightly salted, is taken as a draft. It brings on excessive evacuations to the point of causing an extraordinary thinness. The invalid rids himself of everything bad he had in his body, regains an iron health and (a wondrous thing) acquires excellent eyesight.

Ostrich fat is sold in the markets and a supply of it is laid in in the tents of distinction to give to the poor as a remedy. Moreover, it is not very expensive, as a pot of ostrich fat can be exchanged for only three pots of butter.

The ostrich plumes are sold in the *kuesours*, in Touggourt,[2] in Laghouat,[3] and among the Beni-Mzab who, at the time of buying grain, bring the products of the ostrich as far as the coast.[4]

Among the Oulad Sidi-Chikh the products from the male (*délim*) are sold for from four to five *douros* and those of the female (*reumda*) for two or three *douros*. In the Sahara before we French came, no use was made of the beautiful plumes of the ostrich other than to decorate the tops of the tents or the tops of straw hats.

The Chamba (a Saharian tribe) strengthen their footgear with the soles of the ostrich's feet. They put a piece under the toe and another under the heel and the slipper thus gives very good service. With the tendons they make long narrow thongs to sew saddles, reinforce objects made of leather, etc.

The chase of the ostrich has for the Arab the double attraction of profit and pleasure. It is a sport greatly enjoyed by the horsemen of the Sahara; but it is also a fruitful enterprise. The price of the products and the fat greatly compensate for the expenditures.

Despite the amount of equipment necessary to undertake the chase of the ostrich, the rich man is not alone in being able to permit himself to indulge in it. The poor man who feels himself capable of coming out well from the undertaking finds a means to join himself to hunters chasing the ostrich. He goes to seek an affluent Arab. The latter lends him the camel, the horse, its tack, two-thirds of the barley necessary for the expedition, two-thirds of the goatskins, two-thirds of the pro-

---

[2] Touggourt: town of the Sahara, capital of a small state formed by the thirty-five villages of the oasis called Oued-Rir, sixty-six leagues from Biskra.
[3] Laghouat: seventy-nine leagues southwest of Biskra. A town of seven to eight hundred houses.
[4] See *Le Sahara Algérien* for the two localities in notes 2 and 3.

visions of food. The borrower furnishes the other third of the necessary equipment and the fruits of the chase are divided in the same proportions.

The servant who, during the expedition, has ridden the camel lent to the poor man receives two *boudjous* for each male killed and one *boudjou* for each female. He is, moreover, fed on the rations brought along by the horseman.

Hunting the Ostrich from Blinds

The ostrich is hunted from blinds when it has laid its eggs, that is to say toward the middle of the month of November. Five or six horsemen, taking with them two camels loaded with enough supplies for a month at least, start off in search of places where it has rained recently, where there are pools. Assuredly there, there will be found abundant pasture which will have attracted a large number of ostriches.

To cut short useless journeys, everyone is questioned, all the caravans met with in the Sahara, the locations then being known almost exactly.

The hunter arms himself, on this occasion, not with a club but with a rifle and an abundant supply of powder and balls. When they come upon the traces of the ostrich, the hunters study them very carefully. If they are seen only at intervals in places stripped of grasses, they indicate that the ostrich has come to feed in that place. However, if the traces crisscross in all directions, if the grasses have been trampled underfoot and not eaten, the ostrich, with all surety, has its nest in the environs. The hunters actively seek the place where the ostrich might have laid its eggs and approach it with the greatest of precautions.

When the ostrich digs its nest soft cries can be heard all day; after having laid, its customary cry is not uttered until about three o'clock in the afternoon.

The female broods from morning until noon and during that time the male goes to feed. At noon he returns and the female goes to feed in her turn. When she comes back, she places herself at four or five paces from the nest, facing the male, who broods all night. The male himself watches over the eggs to defend them from their enemies. The jackal, among others, often lurks in the vicinity, ready to play some

evil tricks. Hunters have many times found, on the approaches to ostrich nests, the bodies of dead jackals. Only the male could have struck
them, as the female is timid and not to be feared.

It is in the morning, while the female broods, that the hunters go to
dig—on each side and at some twenty paces at the most from the nest
—pits deep enough to hold a man. Each pit is covered over with those
long grasses, so common in the desert, so that only the rifle barrel appears. The best marksmen are placed in these pits.

At the sight of that labor the terrified female runs to join the male.
But he beats her and forces her to return to her nest. If these preparations are made while the male broods he goes to join the female and
neither one of the two [then] returns.

The female having returned to the nest, care is taken not to make
her uneasy. It is a rule to kill the male first; therefore his return from
feeding is awaited. Toward midday he arrives and the hunter gets
ready. The ostrich, on brooding, extends its wings in such a manner
as to cover all the eggs. In that position, bent on its hocks, its thighs
are very extruded, a favorable circumstance for the marksman. He always aims in such a fashion as to break the animal's legs; in that way
it cannot escape him; it would still have a chance to save itself, were it
wounded in another place.

As soon as the ostrich falls, one hastens over to it and it is bled.
The two marksmen emerge from their blinds and their companions,
having come up at the sound of shots, lend a hand with the task. The
bloodstains are covered up with sand and the ostrich's body is carefully
hidden.

At sunset, the female returns as usual to spend the night near her
nest. The absence of the male does not disturb her. She thinks he is
feeding and gets ready to brood. She is killed in the same manner as
the male by a hunter who has not yet fired.

He who has killed the male receives a *douro* over and above his
share; but, if by some very rare chance, he has missed his mark, he pays
his companions the price of the animal.

"We chose you," someone says to him, "as the best marksman. We
placed you in a good position to do us good and then you caused us
such a loss. You shall pay for it."

The hunter who has killed the female only receives an egg over and above his share; if he has not been successful, he is deprived of that which would have come to him from the price of the male and the eggs.

He who is to shoot at the male is designated in advance.

The nest of an ordinary pair of ostriches contains from twenty-five to thirty eggs. But it often happens that many pairs gather together to lay in common. Then they form a large enclosure and the oldest couple lays in the middle, the others surround them in an even formation. Thus, if there are four, they occupy the four corners of a square. The laying over with, the eggs are pushed toward the center, but not mixed up, and when the oldest male comes to brood all the others take their places at the spot where their eggs were laid, as do the females in their turn.

These flocks are composed of the young of the same family; they are the young of the oldest couple. They do not lay so many eggs. The young a year old, for example, lay but four or five eggs and their eggs are smaller. Sometimes as many as one hundred eggs are found in the same nest. These gatherings of many couples are noted only where the grass is very abundant.

The Arabs have noted a quite singular peculiarity: the eggs of each couple, in the nests of which we have just spoken, are arranged in heaps, [which are] always surmounted by one prominent egg which was the first one laid and which has a special purpose. Incubation lasts for ninety nights.

When the male senses that the moment of hatching has arrived he breaks open with his beak the egg he judges to be the farthest along. At the same time, with a great deal of caution, he makes a small opening in the egg surmounting the others. The latter serves as the first meal for all the newly hatched and for that purpose, although open, it keeps for a long time without spoiling. That is the way it must be, for the male does not break open all the eggs on the same day, but only three or four, when he hears the little ones moving. The egg on which the chicks feed is always liquid, be it a provision of nature, be it that instinctively the parents have brooded it badly.

The chicks, after having received their first meal and as soon as they are dried by the sun, start running about. At the end of a few days they follow their father or mother to feed. In the nest they always place themselves under their [parents'] wings.

The nest has a circular shape, it is built in sandy soil. The ostrich makes it with its feet by simply scraping away the sand from the center to the edge. The dust raised by such labor can be seen from very far away.

The hunters eat the eggs if they are fresh and far from the time when they should hatch. Then they throw away the shells or take them with them to give away as presents to friends or to place on a *koubba*.[5] However, for some time now the Arabs have known that eggs would be bought on the coast and they have made a business out of them.

Hunting from blinds is very lucrative, as it is possible to kill many ostriches and carry off their eggs. At the season when it takes place, it is true that the ostrich is very thin, but, on the other hand, the plumes are more beautiful and keep better.

In the case of many couples gathered at the same nest, only the oldest male and female are killed; if as many holes were to be dug as there were ostriches, they would be swiftly discovered and the entire flock would flee.

The ostrich, say the Arabs, kills a viper[6] with a blow from its beak and eats it; it also eats serpents, insects, grasshoppers, scorpions, lizards, and some large fruit called *hadj*, abundant in the desert and borne by a creeping plant, bitter as terebinth, with leaves similar to those of the melon.[7] In a word, the ostrich even swallows stone. The voracity of that bird is such that, in the places where it is kept captive, it bolts everything it can find—knives, women's jewels, bits of iron. The Arab who

[5] *Koubba:* a small, square chapel surmounted by a dome in which a Marabout is ordinarily buried. It is almost always a stopping place for solitary travelers.

[6] This is the carpet viper (*Echis carinata*). Its native name is *lefâ*. Its habitat extends over a wide area, including the sandy areas of North Africa, and it is greatly feared everywhere as it is inclined to bite. It is beautifully marked and one of the most venomous of the vipers, altogether an unusual snake. It moves in a mobile, double spiral and this peculiar form of locomotion enables it to move over loose sand with considerable confidence and with the advantage of being at all times coiled and ready to strike. (*Reptile Life*, Zdeněk Vogel, translated by Margot Schierl.) [Translator's note]

[7] This is the fruit of the colocynth vine which is allied to the watermelon. It is also called bitter apple, bitter cucumber, bitter gourd. A powerful cathartic is prepared from the fruit. [Translator's note]

furnished me these details related that one day a woman had her coral necklace plucked off and swallowed by an ostrich, and I have heard an army officer in Africa affirm that one of those animals had torn off and eaten one of the buttons from his tunic. The ostrich is at the same time so skillful that it can take a date from between a man's lips without injuring him.

When the lightning flashes, heralding a storm, the ostrich cannot contain itself for joy. It gambols and runs rapidly toward the water it loves so much, although it can endure thirst for a long time.

The mating season for the ostrich is the month of August. The female turns very coy; the male, furious with passion, follows her sometimes for four or five days. He does not drink, he does not eat, and he moans constantly. Finally, when the female is at the end of her resistance, she places herself in the same position as when she broods and the male treads her. As soon as the union has been consummated, the female wants never to separate herself from the male; she never leaves him until the time when the young are grown. Stallions battle for mares, camels for she-camels, but male ostriches never fight over their females. The love affairs of each couple are respected by all.

Paternal love is carried to great lengths by the ostrich; he never abandons his young, he never fears danger, of whatever kind it may be —be it dog, hyena, even man. The female, on the contrary, swiftly becomes frightened and abandons everything when terrified. Thus, when it is desired to speak of a man who firmly defends his tent, he is compared with a *délim*; a weak man is compared to the female ostrich, to the *reumda*.

Ordinarily one encounters ostriches traveling in couples or in a flock of four or five couples. However, at the place where rain has fallen one is sure of finding two or three hundred of them. From a distance they appear to be herds of camels.

Never will the ostrich approach inhabited places, except to drink, and then it flees immediately.

The Arabs hunt the young of the ostrich. The method is very simple; once on their tracks and at a short distance from the ostriches, they utter yells. The startled little ones take refuge close to the father

or the mother, who halts; and then the hunters come up, in defiance of
the male, to capture the young in front of his eyes. The *délim* then
becomes excessively agitated, he displays the most extreme sorrow.
Sometimes salukis are used for that type of hunting. The ostriches defend themselves against them. During the struggle the men carry off
the young without any hindrance and raise them in their tents.

These young ostriches are easily tamed. They play with the children
and sleep under the tent. During the moves from one place to another
they follow the camels. There is no example of one of them having
been raised thus having fled. They are very playful, they gambol with
the horsemen, the children, the dogs. Should a hare go by, all the men
give chase, the ostrich arouses itself, rushes toward the hunt and takes
part in it. When it encounters in the *douar* a child having something
to eat in its hand, it gently knocks the child down and tries to carry
off what the child was holding. The ostrich is very thieving or, rather,
as I have said, it wants to gulp down everything it sees; thus, the Arabs
are suspicious of it when they are counting money. It would swiftly
cause two or three *douros* to disappear.

It is not unusual to see, at some distance from the *douar*, a tired
child placed on the back of an ostrich which bears its burden straight
to the tent, the small rider hanging on to the tips of the wings. But it
will not carry a heavier burden, a man, for example. It throws the
burden off with a blow from its wing. During a journey, when it is
desired to keep the ostrich from running here and there, a cord is tied
around its hocks and it is restrained with another cord attached to the
first.

In the desert the ostrich has no enemy to fear other than man. It
resists the dog, the jackal, the hyena, the eagle. Man alone triumphs
over it.

I have spoken of a third method of hunting the ostrich when it goes
to slake its thirst. The Arabs simply dig a pit close to the water, wait
in ambush, and fire on the animal when it comes to drink.

The hunting of the ostrich in the Sahara makes for numerous excellent marksmen. They make an effort to hit only the head so that the
blood will not stain the plumes. A renowned marksman always car-

ries a small rosary of talismans behind the battery of his rifle and his name is cited among the tribes. Zaatcha[8] numbered more than one celebrated ostrich hunter among its defenders.

The ostrich drinks every five days, more or less, when there is water; if not, it can endure thirst for a very long time.

The hunting of the ostrich is regarded as being highly profitable. The Arabs say of a good business transaction: "It is a good deal, it is like the hunting of the ostrich."

The Arab who has given me these details is an Oulad-Sidi-Chikh, named Abd-el-Kader-Mohammed-ben-Kaddour; his profession is that of hunter. According to him, ostrich country is that comprised in the rectangle from Insalah (El Touât) to Figuig, from south to north; from Figuig to Sidi-Okba, from west to east and, lastly, from Sidi-Okba to Ouargla, from north to south.

[8] Zaatcha was a fortified town and oasis in the province of Constantine. It was the scene of an uprising against the French in 1849 due to a dispute over a tax on palms. The French besieged and finally took Zaatcha, giving no quarter. There was not even an approximate number (estimated) of the dead lying in its streets and there were only a handful of survivors.

8

THE CHASE OF THE GAZELLE

The days of the chase do not
count among the days of life.

The chase of the gazelle is not, like that of the ostrich, a lucrative, and at the same time grueling, enterprise. It is an exercise, a game, a pleasure outing. The gazelle is scarcely worth a franc or a franc and a half and it is not for a quarry of such feeble price that an Arab will prepare, train, and tire a horse whose loss he risks, as frequently comes to pass in the case of the ostrich.

Furthermore, in that chase [of the gazelle], the principal task does not fall to man or to the horse for whom it is, properly speaking, but an outing; it belongs to the saluki, that other companion of the noble horseman of the desert, of which I shall not be long in speaking.

For the rest, if the gazelle is of such little worth, it is not rare. Everywhere, but principally on the Sersou [plateau], is found the *sine* or small gazelle; in the Tell and the mountains *el ademi*, the largest species. *El rinne*, the intermediary species from the point of view of height, is found in the Sahara. It can be recognized from the whiteness of its belly and haunches and the length of its horns.

All of them travel in herds of from four, five, ten, twenty, thirty, and one hundred. Sometimes there are found, even quite frequently, as many as two or three hundred gathered together. From a distance it could be imagined that one is looking at the herd of a migrating tribe. A herd of gazelles is called *djelliba*.

The hunting of the gazelle is not a pleasure reserved exclusively for horsemen. In the migrations of a tribe which are renewed daily in the Sahara, once camp has been set up near a spring, a river, hunters depart in large numbers, taking care to travel against the wind. The gazelle has a keenly developed sense of smell, the scent of man which the wind carried to it would cause it to flee at once.

The hunter advances by hiding behind one bush after the other, imitating the cry of the gazelle from time to time. The latter halts, looks all around, seeking its strayed companion. The hunter gets close to it, he can be seen without its fleeing. At a suitable distance he fires one shot. Rarely does he miss "unless a spell cast on his weapon does not permit him to make a long shot or prevents him from firing all day." At the sound of the shot, the entire herd flees swiftly. At a league or a league and a half [away] their fright has vanished, the memory of what caused their alarm has been lost, they stop to graze as before.

The true hunter is vigorous, an untiring walker; his infallible instinct reveals to him the place where the herd will stop. He goes toward it, goes into concealment again, and renews the chase. He can, thus, in one day kill three or four gazelles which his friends and his servants will retrieve and glory in taking back to the camp.

In the spring, when the small *djedi* (fawns) sleep in the *alfa*, full of their mothers' milk, sometimes twelve or fifteen are taken in a morning. Most often, it is their mothers who betray them.

Chasing the Gazelle on Horseback

The sport of the man of distinction, of the gentleman, does not lie in the foregoing. What the great personages permit themselves is coursing. Twelve or fifteen horsemen go on an expedition. They take with them servants, tents, provisions, and seven to eight salukis and they travel toward the country where the gazelles are ordinarily to be found.

From then on travel is at random. When a herd of gazelles is seen in the distance one goes toward it, keeping as concealed as possible by means of trees and the brokenness of the terrain. Arrived at the distance of about one quarter of a league away, the servants, who had the dogs on a leash and had held their muzzles to prevent their excited barking, dismount and loose them. Scarcely unleashed they speed like arrows and the Arabs excite them even more by yells and frightful invocations: "My brother! My lord! My friend! There they are!"

The horsemen follow them without haste, at a canter and in such a manner as not to lose their tracks; behind come the supplies.

The best salukis do not reach the midst of the herd until after a run of two or three leagues. It is only then that the spectacle truly has incidents and interest. The purebred saluki singles out the most beautiful animal in the herd and hurls himself upon it. Battle is joined, a battle of speed and skill. The gazelle whirls, plunges to left and right, bounds forward, backward, even leaps over the saluki, now seeks to have its traces lost, now seeks to gore the dog. But all its movements will not save it; untiring, ardent, its enemy presses. At the moment of being overtaken, the gazelle bellows, utters plaintive sounds; it is its death song, it is the victory song of the saluki which launches itself and with one bite behind the head breaks the vertebra. The gazelle falls and lies motionless under the eyes of its vanquisher, until the hunters come up and swiftly bleed the still living animal.

Each time, as every good believer should put himself in good order, that he does not arrive until an hour after the gazelle has been brought down, before loosing the dogs, he will not have forgotten to say: "*Bessem Allah, Allah ou kebeur* (In the Name of God, God is the mightiest)." For the Prophet has said: "When you have loosed your dog and you have invoked the Name of God, if your dog has kept for you the game he captured and you have found it still alive, cut its throat to purify it,[1] and if it is dead when you come upon it and your dog has not eaten of it, eat it."

If the invocation has been omitted through forgetfulness, the game may be eaten. It may not be if the omission was voluntary.

Well-mounted horsemen, masters of the best salukis, renew the chase and it is only in the evening that animals and men rest.

Sometimes the hunters eat the gazelle at the place where they have

[1] So that the purification be complete, it is necessary that the esophagus, the the tracheal artery, and the two jugulars be cut.

set up their camp; sometimes on return the following day to the *douar* they send the fruits of their hunting to their relatives, to their friends, and it is an occasion for festivities and family parties for which the flesh of the gazelle, highly regarded by the Arabs, forms the main dish.

Gazelles are raised in the tents; they travel with the sheep during moves, but they always end playing false (escaping).

Winter is the true season for the chase of the gazelle and the antelope. The earth, soaked by heavy rains, slows and hinders their course and, too, the horses and dogs find water everywhere. In the snowy season when an Arab party falls on a herd of gazelles it causes a veritable carnage. At that season the gazelles cannot run; they are famished and easy to overtake. A man sometimes kills ten or fifteen.

For the chase of the gazelle the Arabs wear three burnooses, boots with slippers inside, and carry the horse's blanket under the saddle.

The gazelle gives birth twice a year. The first takes place toward the end of February. In season the female is coy and must be pursued sometimes one or two days before yielding.

The proverbial beauty of their eyes and the whiteness of their teeth have given rise to some quite singular practices. Pregnant women have a gazelle brought before them to lick its eyes as they are persuaded that the eyes of the [unborn] child will be like them. They touch the gazelle's teeth with a finger and then rub it in their mouths.

The horns of the gazelle, filed down and silver-mounted, are used as pins to put *koheul* on the eyes, and the hide, carefully tanned, is made into *mezoueud* (cushions) in which the women keep their most precious possessions.

THE SALUKI (*Slougui*)

What! You, a purebred *slouguia,* you have
prostituted yourself to the low born! It is
infamous! Your crime shall die with you.

If there is still need of demonstrating how very aristocratic the customs
of the people of the Sahara are, how their tastes are the tastes of great
gentlemen, I shall give a very simple proof of it. Certain people might
find it puerile, perhaps. It is the affection shown to the saluki.

In the Sahara, as in other Arab lands, the dog for man is nothing
but a scheming rascal, importunate, rejected, notwithstanding the use-
fulness of his task, be it that he guard the *douar* or watch over the
flocks.

Only the saluki has the esteem, the consideration, the watchful tenderness of his master. That is because the rich, as well as the poor,
regard him as a companion of their chivalresque pastimes in which
they take such pleasure. For the poor, the saluki is also the purveyor
who keeps them alive. Thus he is not trained with hurried pains. His
breeding is supervised with the same precautions as that of the mare.
In the Sahara a man will travel from twenty-five to thirty leagues to
mate a beautiful bitch with a renowned dog. And a renowned dog
takes the gazelle on the run.

"When he sees a gazelle cropping off a blade of grass he overtakes
it before it has time to swallow what it has in its mouth." That is hy-

perbole and that which I have said in the preceding chapter is proof of it, but that hyperbole has its reason for being.

If by some fatal chance a bitch (*slouguia*) has mated with a watchdog, she is made to abort by massaging the young in her belly when they are formed, or else the young are cast off as soon as they have seen the light of day. But it is not only her maternal affection which is threatened; it is, moreover, her life which is at stake through a *mésalliance*. Often the owner, furious upon learning that one of his bitches has been sullied by contact with a shepherd's dog, mercilessly puts her to death.

"What!" he cries. "You, a purebred bitch, you have prostituted yourself to the lowborn! It is infamous! Your crime shall die with you!"

Greatness has its sorrows.

The bitch having whelped, the puppies are never out of sight for an instant. The women themselves sometimes give them their own milk. Visitors arrive, the more numerous and the more respectful the greater the bitch's repute. Her master is surrounded, he is offered milk, *couscous*; there is no form of flattery [which is not] thrust upon him in order to obtain a saluki puppy.

"I am your friend, I pray you, give me what I ask; I will accompany you on your hunts. . . ."

To all these requests the owner ordinarily replies that he will not fix his choice of the puppies which he wishes to keep until the end of seven days. That reserve is motivated by one of the most singular observations that the Arabs make. After a saluki bitch has whelped one of the puppies will always crawl on top of the others. Is it vigor? Is it simple chance? To make sure, the puppy is removed from its usual place, and if, for seven consecutive days, it crawls back, the owner bases such great hopes on it that he would not exchange it for a Negress.

An established prejudice causes to be regarded as the best of the litter those puppies which arrive first, third, or fifth—the uneven numbers.

The puppies are weaned at the end of forty days. They are still given, however, goat's or camel's milk, mixed with dates or *couscous*.

Flocks are so numerous in the Sahara and milk there is in such great abundance that it is not astonishing to see wealthy Arabs, after having weaned their saluki puppies, give them nannies to suckle.

When the young salukis are three or four months old, attention to their training begins. The children chase jerboas or rats called *boualal* out of their burrows and launch the young salukis on them. A short time later the salukis warm to that type of hunting and follow the little animals, barking around the entrances to their refuges until the children renew the exercise.

At [the age of] five or six months comes the matter of a quarry more difficult to overtake—the hare. Someone on foot leads the saluki close to where the animal is crouched that the dog is to overtake. With a slight exclamation the young dog is alerted and throws itself on the hare, rapidly acquiring the habit of [making] a swift and intelligent course.

From the hare, progress is made to the young of the gazelle. Approach is made to the places where they are lying close to their mothers. The saluki's attention is drawn and, as soon as he is well animated, when he strains with impatience, he is loosed. After a few tries the saluki succeeds perfectly and begins to warm to the pursuit of the does.

Those first lessons ended, the saluki has become a year old. He is then almost at the height of his development. His sense of smell is keen, he scents the spoor of the gazelle. He is always carefully rated, scarcely being allowed to hunt until he is fifteen or eighteen months old. But from that time forward he is kept leashed and there is great trouble stopping him for, say the Arabs, when the saluki scents game his muscular power is such that, should he plant his feet, a man can scarcely make him lift a foot.

When he perceives a herd of thirty or forty gazelles the saluki quivers with joy. He gazes at his master, who says to him: "Ah! Son of a Jew. You shall not tell me this time that you did not see them."

The hunter then removes his goatskin and cools the back, belly, and private parts of the saluki. The saluki, impatient, turns a supplicating eye on his master. At last! He is free! He bounds, conceals himself; he crouches if he is seen, follows an oblique course, and it is not until he is within range that he launches himself full force and chooses as a victim the most beautiful male in the herd.

When the hunter cuts up the gazelle he gives the saluki the flesh around the kidneys; if he is given intestines, the dog will disdainfully reject them.

The saluki which, when two years old, does not know how to hunt, will never know. In that regard it is said:

> *Slougui men bad haouli,*
> *ou radjel men bad soumeïn.*
> (The saluki after two years
> And the man after two fasts,
> If they are not worth anything,
> There is no hope.)

The saluki is intelligent and full of self-esteem. When he is loosed, and after a beautiful doe has been indicated to him he has killed but a small one, of mediocre appearance, he is very sensitive to reproaches, he goes away ashamed without reclaiming his share.

Vanity is not lacking in him. "He makes a great deal of *fantasia* [show]." A purebred saluki neither eats nor drinks from a dirty vessel; he refuses milk into which someone has plunged his hands. Has he not been trained for delicate disdain? Whereas the common dog, useful and vigilant guardian, is at the most allowed to seek his food among carrion and old bones, whereas he is shamefully repulsed far from the tent and the table, the saluki, he, himself, lies in the room reserved for the men, on the carpets at his master's side or even on his bed. He is clothed, protected from the cold with blankets like the horse; it is well known that he is very sensitive to the cold. It is one more proof of his being purebred. Pleasure is taken in adorning him, in putting shell collars on him. He is protected against the evil eye by the talismans put on him. He is fed carefully, with concern, also with precaution. *Couscous* is given to him liberally. In summer to give him strength a *pâtée*, made of milk and dates with their pits removed, is made for him. There are some who never feed their salukis in the day-time.

However, that is not enough. The saluki accompanies his master on

his visits; like him he is given hospitality (*difa*) and has his share of
each dish. A purebred saluki never hunts but with his master. He
knows, by his cleanliness, his respect for conventions, and the gracious-
ness of his manners, how to acknowledge the consideration of which
he is the object. He never fails to dig a hole to defecate and then to
cover it over. At his master's return, after a slightly prolonged absence, the saluki, in a single bound, launches himself from the tent
onto the saddle and caresses him.

The Arab talks to him: "O my friend! Listen to me. It is necessary
that you bring me some meat; I am weak from eating nothing but
dates," and a thousand flatteries. The saluki leaps, frisks about; he has
the air of having understood and wanting to reply.

The death of a saluki is [a cause of] mourning for all the tent;
women and children weep for him as for a member of the family. It
is he, sometimes, who supplies the food for all. The saluki who feeds
a family is never sold; sometimes he is given away at the supplications
of women, relatives, or venerated Marabouts.

The saluki who easily takes the *sine* and *el ademi* is worth a beautiful she-camel; he who overtakes the *rinne* is rated as being worth a
prize horse.

Ordinarily the salukis are named *ghrezal* or *ghrezala* (gazelle).

Often betting factions are formed in favor of this or that saluki. The
stakes are ordinarily sheep, feasts, etc.

The saluki of the Sahara is much superior to that of the Tell. He is
of a tawny color, tall, with a long narrow muzzle, wide forehead,
short ears, muscular neck, very pronounced haunch muscles, no belly,
clean legs, tendons prominent, hocks close to the ground, sole little
developed, dry, the upper forelegs very long, the palate and tongue
black, the hair very soft.

Between the two ilia there should be room for four fingers; it is
necessary that the tip of the tail, brought under the thigh, reach the
bone of the haunch.

Ordinarily five lines of fire are applied to each foreleg to consolidate
the joints.

The most renowned salukis in the Sahara are those of the Hamyâne,
the Oulad-Sidi-Chikh, the Harrar, the Arbâa and the Oulad-Naïl.

10

HAWKING WITH A FALCON (*Thaïr el Horr*)

Yes! I swear to you by the Head of the Prophet that, next to a goum starting off on a campaign, nothing is as splendid as a departure for, or return from, hawking.

The hunting equipment of a noble in the Sahara is complete when he has a pedigreed bird, *thaïr el horr*; in the Sahara men of means still hunt with falcons.

The *thaïr el horr* is a dark yellow color; it has a short, strong beak, thick, well-muscled thighs, and sharp talons. It is very rare. Here is the method used to capture it: When a *thaïr el horr* has been sighted, a domestic pigeon is placed inside a species of small net. It is thrown into the air in front of the bird of prey; the latter falls on it, but its talons become entangled in the net, it cannot retract them or escape and it is captured. When the falcon finds itself enmeshed it gives no sign of anger or fright and there exists a proverb in the desert which is repeated in times of misfortune: *"Thaïr el horr ila haseul ma iqtrebochi* (A pedigreed bird, when captured, does not become downcast)."

Rings are placed on its feet and it is tied to a small perch which has been prepared for it in the tent. To accustom it to man, its head is covered with a hood, permitting only the beak to emerge. People speak in its presence and, when the hood is removed, its master gives it fresh meat, holds it on his wrist, strokes it, and speaks to it, as much as possible in a considerable gathering, so as to accustom it to noise. At the end of a month the bird recognizes its master and is completely tame.

Then one takes a young hare, tied by one leg—the falcon also being tied with a very long cord, unhooded—and the hare is turned loose in front of it. The instant the bird perceives it, it soars, uttering cries. The hare stops and crouches, the falcon swoops upon it and kills it with a blow from its feet. The owner hastens up, guts the hare, and gives a part of it to the falcon to eat. That exercise is repeated just until the bird demonstrates that it has no desire to escape and waits for its master close to the slain hare.

The falcon—always inclined to carry off its prey—is considered trained when it answers to recall before or after having seized the game. Arrived at that stage the bird may be taken on a hunt. Its master mounts and carries it with him, hooded, on his head or on his shoulder. He removes the hood, arousing the bird with his voice, the instant he sees a hare. The falcon soars in the air, plummets downward uttering cries and kills it with one blow. It is immediately rehooded.

Sometimes the hare is killed very far from the hunter. It cannot be bled in time to accord with religious formula but the difficulty is obviated upon saying when the bird is loosed: "Bessem Allah, Allah ou kebeur (In the Name of God, God is the Mightiest)." If the falcon has eaten part of the game the rest may be eaten by the hunter, because that bird of prey has been trained to return to its master when he recalls it and not not to eat the game.

A pedigreed bird can kill the hare, the rabbit, the young of the gazelle, the habara (a bird as large as the stork),[1] the pigeon, and the dove.

Only the djouad (nobles) go hawking. These are gatherings of twenty-five or thirty personages and stakes are wagered.

A falcon is paid for with a camel, with one hundred boudjous, sometimes with a horse.

The tribes of the Sahara who still go hawking are: in the east, the Douaouda, the Selmya, the Oulad-Moulat, the Oulad-ben-Aly, they are reputed as nobles among the tribes of the desert; in the west, the

[1] The habara would appear to me to be the guinea fowl.

Oulad-Sidi-Chikh, the Harrar, the Hamyâne, and the Angades. That kind of hunting is also frequent in the Tell, on the edge of the Sahara. The pedigreed bird, like the eagle, does not eat carrion.

The falcon is always in the tent; it is the object of the most attentive care. There are chieftains who never separate themselves from their falcons but take them everywhere with them. It is a mark of distinction, of gentility, if I may dare to say so, to have on the burnoose the traces of the falcon's mutes.

OBSERVATIONS OF THE EMIR ABD-EL-KADER

The Pedigreed Bird

The Arabs recognize four species of pedigreed birds (*thaïr el horr*) which they use for hawking. They are: *el berana*; *el terakel* (peregrine falcon); *el nebala*; *el bahara*. The *berana* and the *terakel* are the most esteemed; above all, the *terakel*, which is the largest and of which the female sometimes attains the size of an ordinary eagle.

The *terakel* has black wings, gray feathers under the wings, black and white breast, black tail, black head (when young), which turns gray and then white as it grows older. Its beak is very strong and very sharp; its talons are solid and active. The *berana* is a little less powerful and of a smaller size than the *terakel*. The wings are grayish white, the breast white, the tail gray and white, with white predominating. The head is multicolored with white still predominant. The *bahara* is almost entirely black except for some white tints on the breast. "It is a Negro, it is not worth very much." The *nebala* is predominantly gray, with some white tints on the wings. It has yellow feet. All these birds molt at the end of summer.

The pedigreed bird is sold less often than it is given away. Someone who has captured one takes it to the master of a large tent who makes the giver a present.

It is during the summer that an attempt is made to capture the pedigreed bird, *thaïr el horr*, in order to have time to train it for hawking toward the end of autumn. Here is the method used to capture it: A pigeon is covered with a type of shirt made of horsehair and leftover wool. A horseman, carrying that pigeon, goes to roam deserted places and throws it in the air when he sees a pedigreed bird. Then he goes to hide. The falcon swoops down upon the pigeon and seizes it, but its talons and feet become enmeshed in the horsehair and wool; it struggles and becomes more and more entangled. At the end of its efforts, worn-out, exhausted, it ends by descending or rather, falling to earth. The hunter emerges from his hiding-place and captures it.

Once it has been captured, a perch is erected in the tent of the chieftain himself and the bird is tied with an elegant cord of *filály* (leather worked in Tafilelt);[2] it is unnecessary to say that the jess is fastened on with the greatest of precaution in order not to wound the bird or irritate it to excess.

It is the master of the tent himself who, every day, once a day toward two o'clock in the afternoon, feeds the bird. The customary food is raw mutton, very clean, and carefully cut up. Food is abundant, the bird can feed to satiation. It should even gain weight.

To train it, one proceeds in the following manner: A piece of meat is presented whole, on making a call with the voice, repeated three times, which might be represented by this drawn-out diphthong: "*ouye, ouye, ouye.*" The bird will fall upon the piece of meat, which is not yielded to it, but which it makes an effort to tear away. Gradually the distance is increased, always presenting the meat to the bird and provoking that unfruitful struggle. Then, at last, before the bird becomes completely worn out, the food is given to it on the perch, cut up into many pieces. The bird will have been, up to that point, always kept inside the tent. It is kept hooded during the day and for the first few nights until it is tame with the women, the children, the animals, the dogs; that latter point is difficult and is never wholly achieved.

When the pedigreed bird has reached that stage, when it is used to receiving its food on the perch, in the manner described, its radius of captivity is widened and to its foot is attached a soft, supple, camelhide thong with a length of fifty or sixty yards, which allows it to emerge, and outside the tent the training of calls to give it some food is tried and repeated, always with a prudent gradualism. It is taken care of thus under the tent for a long time and not taken outside except to be fed. When its master is sure of thus having made it used to him, he

2 *Filály:* goatskins, most often dyed red, prepared in Tafilelt, in Morocco. It is what we call morocco leather.

carries it on his wrist to a quite great distance, putting on and removing its hood at intervals; it is not without difficulties, without contests, that the bird is accustomed to the sight of the outdoors. Nonetheless, it will accustom itself with time.

At that stage the taming of the pedigreed bird is concluded—that is to say that, with the same calls, the same repetitions, but far from the tent and the *douar*, without hood or leash, it is fed. As soon as it is replete, the hood and leash are replaced. Then, at that time, its master carries it everywhere on his wrist.

But, that is not all. The animal has only been tamed. It is necessary to train it for the chase, and here is the manner in which it is done: A hare is taken, it is bled at the throat, the wound is well exposed by drawing back some of the skin so that the flesh appears. Then in the tent, a call is made, after having removed the hood of the *thaïr el horr*, which springs at the hare's neck. It is allowed to become somewhat excited so that it will acquire a taste for hare and that day it is given some of its flesh to eat. That operation is repeated for seven or eight successive days, with a live hare whose ears are pulled to make it cry out, while the bird's master utters the *"ouye, ouye, ouye"* of call. The falcon falls on the hare's head, struggling for it and then it eats the eyes and sometimes the tongue. The hare is opened and the falcon is given some of it to eat. That exercise is repeated more or less frequently, according to the degree of facility the bird has for learning.

The hunting season approaches; it is necessary to test the bird to learn if it has profited by these lessons, so prudently graduated, by such laboriously careful training, so appropriate to its nature and to the kind of pleasure for which it is destined. One goes out, then, on horseback. The pedigreed bird is carried along, hooded. Arrival is made at an open plain or a vast plateau. Five or six live hares are furnished. Arrived on the chosen terrain, the legs of one of the hares are all broken, then it is loosed within sight of the bird. Plaintive and crying out, the hare runs as best it is able; then the hood is removed and the bird loosed, with the cry, *"Bessem Allah, Allah ou kebeur."*

The *terakel*, impatient, soars straight toward the sky and from very far up it swoops down upon the hare which it kills or stuns with a blow from its retracted talons, like a blow from a fist. One draws near the hare, it is bled, opened and the entrails, liver and heart are given to the bird to eat on the spot. After many successive days during which that test is repeated the pedigreed bird is completely trained.

That training is prolonged from summer toward the end of autumn. It is the appropriate season, for the bird does not hunt well except during the time of mists and even cold. It cannot withstand the sun, thirst, heat. It will leave its master to go to seek the water which it has perceived from very far away and will not come back again.

At that season a start is made after a light breakfast toward eleven o'clock in the morning, the pedigreed bird on the shoulder or on the wrist. Only a supply of camel's milk in goatskins, dates, *deglet en nour*, bread, and sometimes dried raisins are carried along. But the chase does not begin until after a quite long course, toward three o'clock in the afternoon. The horsemen are numerous. Arrived at the site of the chase they disperse and beat the thickets, the tussocks of *alfa*, to flush a hare which they then endeavor to beat back toward him who has the falcon. As soon as the game is sighted he removes the hood from the bird and looses it, on pointing out the hare with a finger and saying to it:

"*Ha houa!* (There it is!)"

While its master pronounces the sacramental "*Bessem Allah, Allah ou kebeur* (In the Name of God, God is the Mightiest)," words destined to sanctify the game which has not been bled in order that it be a dish permitted to the true believer, the bird soars off, makes a point almost out of sight while following the hare with its keen vision, then it swoops and strikes it, be it on the head, be it on the shoulder with a blow from its clenched talons, violent enough to stun or even kill it. The horsemen who saw the bird plummet come up from all sides, surround it and usually find it busy eating the hare's eyes. To make it relinquish the game a hare's skin is drawn from the burnoose and thrown down a little farther off on which the bird pounces. It is not until once back in the *douar* that the bird is given its quarry.

It can be understood that if food was abundant, even excessive, at the period when it was desired to tame the bird and derive some benefit from it, it is, on the contrary, well controlled during the entire hunting season, in order not to make the bird clumsy; not to deprive it of its faculties, to make it, in a word, a good hunter, that is to say, spirited and alert. It is not unusual with two or three falcons to kill ten or fifteen hares.

With the *thaïr el horr*, there is also hunted the large bird called the *habara*. That chase takes place in the following manner:

One goes on horseback until some *habara* are encountered, which are found in couples or in companies of four, six, or even more. The falcon is on one's wrist. Its hood is removed, it is shown the *habara*, it is aroused, then released upon enunciating the invocation: "*Bessem Allah.*" The bird soars, then swoops down upon its prey, whose head it grips in its talons where it mercilessly holds it, despite the desperate efforts of the victim, until the horsemen come up and tear it away. One of them bleeds it and gives the falcon its quarry.

That food *intoxicates* the pedigreed bird, say the Arabs, be it because of its perfumed taste, be it because it is proud of the capture of a *habara*, which is a dainty [fit] for a sultan. Thus, when it is replaced on the shoulder, it balances and waddles. "It is making its *fantasia* [show]."

If the *habara* takes wing, the falcon rises. Both rise together. The falcon seeks to dominate it. When it has succeeded, it comes down, breaks a wing and then the breastbone [of the *habara*]. They fall, spinning, but the falcon always manages to keep uppermost and, above all, to get its victim underneath so that only the *habara* will feel the shock of that terrifying descent.

The pedigreed bird, moreover, hunts the *seroun*, the *hama*, the *agad*. There are falcons which do not hunt the *habara*. None of them is trained for the hunting of the partridge. It is feared that getting it used to partridge hunting would lead it to prefer hunting the feather more than the skin.

When a bird tarries in rejoining its master then a horseman, having at hand a hare's skin with ears and legs, which is called *gachouche*, starts off at a gallop in the direction of the bird and throws it the lure, crying out: "*ouye!*" That interjection is, if I may express myself thus, the vocative of the pedigreed bird.

The pedigreed bird, when it is trained, does not often betray its master, that is to say, it is rare that it leaves him. However, some are lost because of a very pronounced taste they have for a desert bird called *hama* which they pursue with frenzy. One wrathfully calls *"ouye!"* and lures are thrown, but they never return.

The *biaz*, as the falconer is called, who is especially charged with caring for and feeding the pedigreed bird, sometimes acquires for his pupil a blind, mournful tenderness. He tends it very carefully and feeds it to excess, even though someone quotes to him the proverb: "Self-esteem is its only counselor, the only motive for its actions, it is not hungry and instead of hunting will regain its freedom."

It is necessary, moreover, that a bird be well trained, even renowned, for it to be kept more than a year. Ordinarily, unless there is signal prowess, it is freed before the hunting season. Departure is made to procure other birds at a favorable time and birds retained for more than three years are cited as exceptional examples.

For the rest, everyone loves them, big or small, rich or poor. How could it be otherwise? We love all that is beautiful, rich, brilliant, magnificent; it is necessary not to be an Arab not to rejoice, not to become excited at the sight of a company of seven or eight noble horsemen returning from hawking. The chieftain rides in the lead. He has two falcons, one on his shoulder, the other on his wrist [which is] covered with a *guefass* (gauntlet).

The hood, *keumbid*, and the jesses are enriched with silk, *filaly*, gold, and small ostrich plumes. The jesses *semaid* are embroidered and ornamented with tiny, silver jingle-bells (*ledjerass*). Next to a *goum* departing for war, nothing is as splendid as the departure to, or the return from, hawking. Although one has been well out of breath, worn out, dead tired; still one is rested, healed, better than by sleep, by the hope of starting again on the following day.

The tribes which hunt with falcons are the Zemonle, Ghiras, Oulad-ben-Embarack, Oulad-Mokran, Oulad-Mady, Oulad-Abdallah, Oulad-Sidi-Ayssa, Oulad-Mokinar, Arbâa, Oulad-Naïl, Oulad-Sidi-Chikh, Metaaria, Oulad-Derradj, Zenakhra, Oulad-Yagoub, Hamyâne, Soua-mâa, and the Oulad-Sidi-Nasser. In a word, all the peoples of Allah.[3]

---

[3] That report is in perfect accord with details drawn from other sources. Sid-Hamed-ben-Mohamed-el-Mokrani, Caliph of the Medjana, and other sheiks of the province of Constantine, presently in Paris, give exactly the same details.

11

THE CHASE

by the Emir Abd-el-Kader

He who has never hunted, or loved, or
swayed to the sound of music, or sought
the perfume of flowers is not a man, he
is an ass.

It is told that an Arab sheik was seated in the midst of a large gathering
when a man, who had just lost his ass, presented himself to the chieftain asking if someone had seen the strayed animal. The sheik turned
toward those who surrounded him and addressed to them these words:
"Is there one among you to whom the pleasures of the chase are unknown? One who has never pursued game with the risk of killing
himself or being injured upon falling from his horse? One who, without fear of rending his garments or his skin, has never launched himself, in order to overtake a wild animal, into thickets bristling with
thorns? Is there one among you who has never felt the pleasure of
finding, the desperation of leaving, a well-loved woman?"

One of his listeners replied: "I! I have never felt or experienced that
which you have just said."

The sheik then regarded the master of the ass. "There!" he said.
"There's the animal you seek; take it away!"

The Arabs say in effect: "He who has never hunted, or loved, or swayed to the sound of music, or sought the perfume of flowers is not a man, he is an ass."

Among us warfare is, before all else, a struggle of agility and wiles; thus the chase is first among pastimes. The pursuit of savage beasts teaches the pursuit of men.

A poet has made the following eulogy to that art: "The chase frees the soul of the cares with which it is encumbered, it adds to the vigor of the intelligence, it brings joy, dissipates woes, and renders useless the skill of doctors upon maintaining a perpetual well-being in the body.

"It makes good horsemen, for it teaches swift mounting into the saddle, prompt dismounting, launching a horse over precipices and cliffs, clearing boulders and bushes at a gallop, galloping without stopping, even when a part of the tack is lost or breaks. The man who devotes himself to the chase makes daily progress in courage; he learns a contempt for accidents.

"To devote himself to his favorite pleasure, he withdraws from wicked men. He ousts gossip and calumny; he evades the corruption of vice; he frees himself from those unfortunate influences which give our beards gray tints and cause to weigh on us, before its time, the weight of the years. The days of the chase are not counted among the days of one's life."

In the Sahara hunting is the only pursuit of the chieftains and wealthy men. When the rainy season arrives the dwellers in that region move themselves to the edges of small lakes formed by the water from heaven, one after another. Just as soon as game begins to become scarce at one place they give their errant lives a new hearth.

A legend, known to all Arabs, proves with what force a passion for hunting can take possession of an African soul: "A man of a great tent fired at a gazelle and missed; in a moment of anger he made an oath not to take any food until he had eaten the liver of that animal. He fired yet once more at the gazelle and did not hit his mark. Nonetheless, he continued his pursuit of it during the day. Night having fallen, his strength failed him, but, faithful to his vow, he took no food. His servants then continued the chase and that chase continued yet three days more. At last the gazelle was killed and its liver was taken to the dying Arab who neared a morsel of that flesh to his lips and then gave his last sigh."

The Arabs hunt on foot and on horseback. A horseman who wants to hunt the hare should take a saluki with him. The gazelle hounds are called *slougui*. They derive their name from Slouguïa, the place where they were first bred, it is alleged, from the coupling of female wolves with dogs.[1] The male saluki often lives for twenty years and the bitch for twelve. The salukis capable of taking a gazelle on a course are very rare. Most of them do not hunt either the hare or the gazelle, even when those animals happen to pass close by them. Their usual quarry is the *bekeur-el-ouhach*[2] which ordinarily they seize by the hock and throw to the ground. It is asserted that that animal, upon trying to get up, falls back on its head and kills itself. Sometimes the saluki seizes it by the neck and holds it until the hunter comes up.

A number of Arabs hunt the *bekeur-el-ouhach* on horseback and strike it from the rear with a lance. It is also on horseback ordinarily that the gazelle is hunted, but a rifle is always used on it. The gazelles live in herds. From the midst of its companions is singled out the one it is desired to kill and it is fired upon without checking the horse, which has been launched into a gallop, for an instant.

An Arab saying goes: "More forgetful than the gazelle." In reality, that beautiful animal, which already has from woman her soft and mysterious gaze, would also appear to have her lightheadedness. The gazelle, when the bullet has missed, runs a little farther away and then stops, insouciant about the lead which, at the end of an instant, comes to seek it again. Some Arabs launch a falcon, trained to attack the eyes, at it.

It is above all among the Arabs of the land of Eschoul where that kind of hunting is the rule. I have encountered there a small tribe,

---

[1] Such a cross is not impossible. Buffon, having seen it, confirms it in documents of an indisputable authenticity. The Jardin des Plantes (see below) possesses one, if not two, carnivorous quadrupeds, born of the union of female wolves with dogs, or of bitches with male wolves. (Jardin des Plantes. This famous Paris institution was founded during the first half of the seventeenth century. Originally only medicinal plants from all over the known world were grown. However, it has been expanded and now has a museum of natural history and a zoological garden.) [Translator's note]

[2] *Bekeur-el-ouhach:* an antelope. [Translator's note]

called the tribe of Es-Lib, which lives only from the products of the chase. The tents there were made of the hides of gazelles and the *bekeur-el-ouhach*; the garments there were, for the most part, but of the remains of wild animals. One of the members of that hunting people told me that he customarily went out with a donkey laden with salt. Each time that he brought down a gazelle, he gutted it, split open the stomach, rubbed the entrails with salt and then left it to dry on a bush. He later retraced his steps and brought back to his family the carcasses which he had thus prepared, for, in that area, there is no carnivorous animal which disputes the game with the hunter. The Es-Lib are so accustomed to eating flesh that their children threw away some biscuits which I had given them. They simply could not imagine that they were something good to eat.

Often hunting from a blind is resorted to against the male and female of the *bekeur-el-ouhach*. When the heat has dried up the lakes of the desert, a hole is dug close to springs and the animals who come to drink find death at the moment of slaking their thirst.

One of the chases demanding the greatest of intrepidity is that of the *lerouy*, an animal which resembles the gazelle but is larger, without always attaining the height of the *bekeur-el-ouhach*. The *lerouy*, which is also called *tis-el-djebel* (mountain goat),[3] keeps itself amid cliffs and precipices. There, it is necessary to pursue it on foot amid a thousand perils. As the animals of that family run very badly an ordinary dog can take them easily as soon as they descend to the plains. But they have, according to what is affirmed, a singular faculty. A *lerouy,* pursued by hunters, can throw itself into a precipice three hundred and fifty feet deep and land on its head without doing itself any hurt. The age of the animal can be confirmed by the rings on its horns; each ring indicates one year. The *lerouy* and the gazelle have two incisor teeth; they do not have teeth (*robaï*) situated between the incisors and the canines.

If the chase of the *lerouy* is the triumph of the man on foot, the chase of the ostrich is the triumph of the horseman. On those days of the sirocco,[4] when a sort of burning sleep seems to weigh upon all na-

---

[3] Mountain goat: This is probably the aoudad or Barbary sheep.
[4] Sirocco: a hot, oppressive, dust-laden wind blowing west from the Libyan deserts.

ture, when it could be believed that all animate beings should be sentenced to rest, intrepid hunters mount their horses. It is known that the ostrich, of all animals the least wily, never deviates but, confiding in it agility alone, flees on a straight, swift course like that of a [straight] line. Five horsemen post themselves at intervals of one league along the line on which it ought to flee; each makes himself a relay. When one halts, the other launches himself at a gallop on the tracks of the animal, which thus cannot find a moment's relaxation and is always struggling against fresh horses. Thus the hunter who takes up the chase last is necessarily the victor. That victory is not unattended by danger. On falling, the ostrich, by the movement of its wings, inspires terror in the horse, which is often fatal to the rider.

On the horses which must perform these great bursts there is placed only one housing and a very light saddle. Some horsemen even use but wooden stirrups and a very light bit, attached by a plain string. The hunter carries with him a small water bag; he moistens the bit from time to time to keep his horse's mouth cool.

But that relay of five riders is not the only method of hunting the ostrich. Sometimes an Arab, who has a profound knowledge of the habits of that game, goes to post himself alone close to a place where an ostrich usually passes by, close to a mountain col, for example; as soon as he sights the animal, he launches himself in pursuit at a gallop. It is rare that he succeeds, for very few horses can overtake an ostrich. I have owned, nonetheless, a mare which excelled in that chase.

Although the horse is usually employed against the ostrich, in that chase, as in all others, it is not, however, an indispensable companion for man. Ruses sometimes take sole charge to combat the ostrich. At the laying season hunters dig holes close to the nests, crouch in them and kill the mother when she comes to visit her eggs. Lastly, the Arabs also have recourse to disguises. Some among them dress themselves in ostrich skins and thus approach the animal they wish to kill. Hunters thus disguised have been, it is said, more than once hit by their companions.

When an ostrich has a leg broken by a bullet it cannot, like other bipeds, hop on only one leg. That is due to the fact that there is no marrow in its bones and that bones without marrow cannot heal when they have been broken. The Arabs affirm that the ostrich is deaf and its senses of sight and smell replace that of hearing.

The hyena is a strong animal whose jaws are dangerous, but it is cowardly and avoids the light of day. It customarily lives in the holes to be found in ravines or cliffs. It ordinarily travels only at night, seeking carrion and cadavers, and commits such depredations in cemeteries that, to prevent them, the Arabs take care to bury their dead very deeply. In certain regions even, two containers are made for the same cadaver, which is placed in the inner one. In general, the hyena does not attack the flocks; however, it sometimes carries off watchdogs during the night around the camps. The Arabs pay little attention to it. They amuse themselves by chasing it on horseback and cause it to be taken by their salukis without rendering it the honor of rifle shots. When the den which the hyena occupies has been well reconnoitered it is not unusual to encounter Arabs, who scorn it enough, boldly penetrating the den after having carefully covered the entrance with their burnooses in order to prevent the least chink of daylight from entering. Having entered, they approach the hyena, speaking to it forcefully; they subdue it, beat it, without its offering the least resistance, so frightened has it become; then they drive it out by means of heavy blows from a club. The hide of an animal so cowardly is little esteemed. In many tents one is not permitted to bring it inside, for it cannot help but bring bad luck. The common people among the Arabs eat the flesh of the hyena which, for the rest, is not good. They take great care not to touch the head, above all, the brain. They believe that that contact would be enough to drive them mad.

We shall leave that ignoble animal aside. There is another, more to be feared; the hunting of which offers moving incidents, although its reputation is far from being in the Arabs' eyes what it is in the minds of Europeans. I wish to speak of the leopard.

The leopard is found everywhere in Algeria. It inhabits only areas with cover; wooded, broken, and difficult. There are many species. Some never leave the region where their lair is established. The Arabs call that species *dolly* (housebound). Others, on the contrary, are those which are called *berrani* (strangers); they frequently leave the district where they sojourn and go to prowl in neighboring districts and even farther afield.

The *dolly* is larger, stronger, and more dangerous than the other species. Its coat is speckled with more evenly distributed spots, some joined to each other, of a very dark shade. The colors are white, black, and yellow. On the cheeks, the four legs, the crest of the back, there are no longer spots, but stripes. Those on the cheeks are diagonally placed, the upper ends start from the lower eyelids, the nostrils, the edges of the lips, descending down the neck, blending into a yellow tone replaced by white.

It usually travels in pairs; in inhabited places it is never seen by day. In those places not inhabited by man, although it comes out by day, it never hunts but at night. It has two or three young. The Arabs are far from having the esteem for the leopard they accord the lion. The lion, they say, if attacked, harried, wounded, surrounded by enemies, feels its courage growing in the midst of noise and at the height of danger; it launches itself freely on its aggressors and fights them relentlessly.

The leopard does not resign itself to battle except when it cannot find any means of retreat. In a word, the lion, as soon as battle is joined, does not evade it; the leopard escapes whenever it can. Another difference is this: the lion devours man, the leopard never does. It will ordinarily strike at the head, rend the man with its claws, inflict terrible bites on him, then, preferring the flesh of other animals to that of the son of Adam, it leaves him and goes in search of other prey. In a land where it can feed on wild boar, sheep, livestock, and game of all kinds, where it contents itself with the carcasses of animals, it does not kill man because it is hungry, but in self-defense; it is ridding itself of an enemy.

For the lion, man is frequently a prey; it goes to hunt him. For the leopard, man is an adversary whom it willingly avoids, whom it takes care not to provoke. Pass confidently and inoffensively by the enormous bush where it lurks and, if you do not attack, it will remain hidden as a quail, holding its breath. But, if you fire at it and miss, it will be on you in one bound and rend and bite; then, little reassured even after having attacked, it will go off.

The Arabs have noted by the number of men who have had engagements with the leopard, and who have only been wounded and not killed, that it rends only with its teeth. Its bite is like that of the dog, it cuts the flesh. The lion, by means of violent shakings, breaks the bones of him whom it has [seized] between its formidable jaws. When the leopard has bitten, without troubling to find out whether or not it has killed, it prudently and timidly goes away. The lion becomes aroused, it attacks repeatedly. The enemy is out of the battle, that is not enough, he shall feel the weight of the lion's rage.

The lion bounds into a *douar*; he thieves boldly, at his ease. He has come to take his share, without concealment. He has nothing to fear, he is exercising his right—the right of the strongest. The leopard dissembles, it glides along, it infiltrates, it creeps like a thief; shame and fear accompany it. The spring of a furious leopard is like lightning; after that immense effort it runs more slowly than a common horse.

A leopard is surrounded, pressed, beaten, befuddled by fear more than by rage; it springs to a tree where marksmen are posted, reaches them. But, at some other moment, if only one or two men are in concealment in a blind, if it is not surrounded on all sides, if the path is open for flight, it forgets its strength, it saves itself. Everywhere and always the lion is a dangerous enemy whose encounter is terrible; it is not until after it has been attacked that the leopard is dreaded.

The cry of the leopard resembles the shrill, clear, powerless bray of the mule, which has nothing frightening about it, compared with the roars of a lion, growling like thunder. But the leopard is agile and quick, its movements are swifter than the eye. Its proverbial suppleness is recalled in this saying:

> *Ida djat el aïn fel aïn*
> *Tekoun chetara fel idain.*

(Should eye meet eye
Celerity shows itself in the wrists.)

If the nature of the leopard leads it to spare man or to avoid him and to choose as prey wild or domestic animals, sheep, cows, gazelles, and antelopes, which do not know how to defend themselves, it leads it also to choose its means of attack against the animals whose way of

life or whose courage make them more difficult or dangerous to over-
come; against the latter the leopard uses surprise by preference. Thus,
it will not go to attack a horse in the midst of a *douar*; its habits of
circumspection, of cowardliness, prevent it from seeking to seize as
prey an animal which could be opportunely rescued or promptly
avenged. Even at pasture a lone horse can elude it by flight, but if the
leopard has been neither seen nor sensed, if in one bound it can spring
on the horse, that horse is lost. Neither is the wild boar an easy victim;
if it is grown, if it has had time and a free field, it successfully defends
itself. Sometimes, even, it is totally the victor and Arabs have found
leopards disemboweled by boars.

A frequent struggle, the only one, perhaps, that the leopard openly
undertakes, takes place between it and the hedgehog (or porcupine);
but, although the latter are large in Africa, appearance is more formidable than reality. The hedgehog has, it is true, the ability to bristle
its long, solid, sharp darts; it can even throw them a certain distance,
but that armor cannot save it. The least wound completely paralyzes the
muscular contractions by means of which it puts itself on the defensive;
furthermore, it needs for that defense some point of support, a stone
or a tree.

However cowardly, however timid the leopard may be, it becomes
really dangerous when its young have been taken by a ruse in its absence; or even in front of it by force, which happens when the hunters
are numerous. Then, sometimes, it causes itself to be killed defending
its young, at least, the *dolly*, that is to say the large species of leopard,
does so. The *berrani*, which is smaller, flees, uttering mournful cries.
The cubs, taken away from their mothers, are given to the chieftains
living in the cities, to the sultans, to the pashas, to the beys. They are
not kept in the tribe. Though young, their games are already dangerous
and all the care imaginable cannot tame them or protect the master of
the tent, his wives, or his children against the possible moment of anger
on the part of the perfidious and capricious animal.

We shall also remark that in certain *zaouïas* [5] some Marabouts tame
lions and wander about with them among the tribes. Thus calling

[5] *Zaouïa:* a religious establishment which ordinarily contains a mosque, a school,
and the tombs of its founders.

curiosity to the aid of charity, they increase the amount of the alms they solicit for their congregation. The most celebrated of the *zaouïas* where tamed lions are kept is that of Sidi-Mohammed-ben-Aouda, a tribe of the Flittas, in the province of Oran.

Save for that very special exception the Arabs (and it is a characteristic custom which should be noted), do not raise any but harmless animals. There is no tent without a gazelle, an antelope, a jackal, an ostrich, a falcon; but not in any *douar* is there to be seen a ferocious animal—hyena, leopard, or lion.

In some tribes, pleasure is taken in raising a small piglet. It is alleged that it is a distraction for the horses, who like its smell. The piglet is faithful; ever in movement, it trots along grunting happily in the midst of the animals of a tribe on the move. It accompanies the calves and the sheep to pasture. It is called the father of good fortune, and, strangely, an encounter with a wild boar upon emerging from the tent is considered a prognostication of good things. The Arabs, before Mohammed, ate pork. It was the Prophet who prohibited it and forbade as well partaking of the blood of animals and of the flesh of any animal dead without having been bled.

The leopard, as I have said, rarely goes out during the day. But if by chance shepherds or travelers encounter it in the vicinity of inhabited places they utter piercing yells of "*Ha houa!* (There it is!)." Those yells are repeated with incredible rapidity. The entire populace turns out, horsemen, men on foot, all armed with whatever they had at hand —rifle, club, saber, lance, pistol—and followed by curs and salukis. The place where the leopard holed up is surrounded—a difficult terrain, covered with high, thick bush. The leopard is openly attacked and ordinarily it is killed. At least it rarely escapes by day.

However, when, instead of that abrupt eruption of an entire populace against the sudden appearance of an enemy, the matter concerns a true hunt, departure is not made without making some preparations.

The leopard, it is true, will flee if it finds an opening. However, it can also come about that it will fight and although, in the final reckoning, it ought to succumb without a man's death, it is a good thing to be forearmed against the wounds it can inflict, even minor ones.

It is the head the leopard has the habit of attacking; against the rendings of the claws and the bites a man is sufficiently protected by a thick cap of wool, the *chachia*, the folds and pleats of the *haïk*, the hood of the burnoose, the numerous coils of the long, stout thong of camelhide. However, as the enemy can, with a bound as rapid as the blink of an eye, spring to the horse's croup and, with a blow of its paw to his head, stun, overthrow, and kill a man, one also wears a helmet, a modest helmet, which is usually a cooking-pot.

The leopard, like the lion, is killed by men lying in wait. A pit is dug in the earth, it is covered over with branches but an opening has been made through which the muzzle of the posted hunter's rifle passes. The leopard is killed at fifteen paces when it comes to devour the carcass of a goat or sheep placed at that distance. But, fearing that the leopard, if it is only wounded, will throw itself upon the *melebda* (the pit which serves the hunter as a blind), the hunter always has two or three rifles and he is also armed with pistols.

Another rifle is tied to a tree. At the tip of that rifle is attached a bait which is, at the same time, tied to a string which, passing around the tree like a pulley, is tied at the other end to the trigger which is pulled when there is a strong tug at the bait. If the leopard is not killed, it is at least wounded, and the hunters start in pursuit guided by the trail of blood.

Finally, the last method of hunting the leopard is to surprise it while it is asleep; it is nothing but a nuisance and not a danger if it is found to be awake, for it flees at the sight of man.

However, whatever may be the type of chase undertaken, even the least timorous [of men] experience the influence of superstitious terrors, as in all enterprises. Such terrors are not sufficient to stop them, if they find themselves in need of starting off, but an attempt is always made to avoid the risks of a sinister augury. On the contrary, a man is emboldened and his hopes are raised when, at the hour of departure, he is saluted by one of those encounters reputed to be lucky: by a jackal in the morning or by a wild boar in the evening.

> May your morning be with a jackal
> And your evening with a wild boar.

A hare or a fox is an omen of bad luck [as is] a lone crow, or a white mare. Even worse, and a more detestable prognostic, is the sight of an old woman.

Good luck to him who sees two crows or a colored mare and, above all, good fortune, glory, booty for the *goum* which, upon departing on an expedition, encounters a beautiful young girl, noble, who bares her bosom and shows one of her breasts. That is the custom and, should she refuse that blessing to the warriors of her tribe, someone [would] dismount to force her [to do so], were she the chieftain's daughter, were he at the head of the *goum*. So much the better if she is of such high birth; the more noble the young girl, the more favorable the omen. In the west the young girl opens her girdle.

If, in the morning, you hear good words, affectionate and polite, the day will be good; bad, if, upon rising you are greeted by an imprecation or an insult. Do not start off on a hunt on a Tuesday, Thursday, or Friday.

Now we come to the chase which, truly, is worth sharpening the wits, inflaming the warriors' souls. The Arab hunter attacks the lion.

There is, in that daring undertaking even more merit, for the lion in Africa is a redoubtable being, on the subject of which there exist a number of mysterious and terrible legends; of which a terrified superstition protects the formidable majesty. With that observant spirit which is their distinctive trait, the Arabs have made on the lion a series of observations worthy of being collected and preserved.

During the day the lion rarely seeks to attack man; ordinarily, even if some traveler passes close to it, it turns its head away and pretends not to see him. However, if some imprudent fellow, skirting a thicket where it is lying, suddenly yells: "He is there! (*Ra hena!*)," the lion springs on him who has just disturbed its rest.

With nightfall the lion's humor changes completely. When the sun has gone down, it is dangerous to venture into wooded, broken, and wild areas. It is there that the lion lies in wait, there where it is found on the paths—which it obstructs by blocking them with its body.

Here are, according to the Arabs, some of the nocturnal dramas then customarily enacted. If a man alone—courier, traveler, letter bearer—who happens to meet a lion has his heart solidly tempered, he goes straight up to the animal, brandishing his rifle or saber but taking care not to fire or strike. He limits himself to crying: "Oh, thief! Cutter of paths! Son of her who never said no! Dost thou think thou canst frighten me? Dost thou not know then that I am a So-and-so, son of a So-and-so? Get up and let me continue on my way."

The lion waits until the man is close to it and then it goes off to lie down again a thousand paces farther on. The traveler is forced to undergo a series of terrifying trials. Each time the lion leaves the path, it disappears, but for a moment only; soon it reappears and in all its maneuvers it is accompanied by a dreadful noise. It breaks innumerable branches in the forest with its tail. It roars, it howls, it grunts, it blows out puffs of pestilential breath. It plays with the object of its multiple and bizarre attacks, holding it continually suspended between fear and hope, like the cat with the mouse. If he who is engaged in that struggle does not feel his courage weaken, if he succeeds, according to the Arabic expression, in controlling his spirit well, the lion will leave him and go seeking luck elsewhere.

If the lion, on the contrary, perceives that it is dealing with a man whose countenance is terrified, whose voice is faltering, who has not dared to utter one threat, it redoubles, to terrify him even more, the tactics described. It approaches its victim, pushes him off the path with its shoulder, obstructs the path at every moment, amuses itself, in short, in every way, until it ends by devouring him half-conscious.

There is nothing incredible, furthermore, in that phenomenon to which all Arabs have attested. The ascendency of courage over animals is an undisputed fact.

According to the Arabs, some of those professional thieves, who travel at night, armed to the teeth, instead of fearing the lion, cry out to it when they encounter each other: "I'm none of thy business! I'm a thief like thou; go on thy way or, if thou likest, let's go to steal together." It is added that sometimes the lion follows them and goes to try a coup at the *douar* to which they direct their steps. It is alleged that this good friendship between lions and thieves is often manifested in a striking way. Thieves have been seen, at mealtimes, treating the lions like dogs and throwing to them at a certain distance the feet and entrails of the animals upon which they nourish themselves.

Some Arab women have also successfully used intrepidity against the lion. They have pursued it at the moment it was carrying off a ewe, and they have made it relinquish its prize by beating it with a stick, accompanying the beating by these words: "Thief! Son of a thief!"

Shame, say the Arabs, then takes possession of the lion, who makes off as fast as possible. To the Arabs that proves that the lion is a sort of creature apart—occupying the space between man and animal—which by reason of its strength appears to them to be endowed with a special intelligence. The following legend, destined to explain why the lion allows the sheep to escape more easily than all its other prey, confirms that opinion:

Upon enumerating what its strength permitted it to do, the lion one day said:

"*An cha Allah* (if God is willing), I shall carry off a horse without hindrance.

"*An cha Allah*, I shall carry off a heifer when I please and its weight will not prevent me from running."

When it came to the ewe the lion thought it so inferior that it neglected the religious formula "if God is willing" and God condemned it, as a punishment, never to be able to carry away a ewe.

There are many methods of hunting the lion.

When a lion appears in the vicinity of a tribe signs of all kinds reveal its presence. First there are roars which make the earth itself seem to tremble; then there are continual depredations, repeated incidents; a heifer, a colt carried off; even a man disappears. The alarm is spread throughout the tents; the women tremble for their possessions and their children; there are complaints from all sides. The hunters decree the death of that disquieting neighbor. A bulletin is posted in the markets that on such and such a day, at such and such an hour, horsemen and men on foot, all men in a condition to hunt will be assembled under arms at a specified place.

The dense thicket where the lion rests during the day has been reconnoitered in advance. Departure is made, the men on foot in the lead. When they arrive at some fifty paces from the thicket where they should encounter the enemy they halt, wait, gather in a body and form three ranks; the second rank being ready to enter the intervals of the front rank if help is needed. The third rank, in close formation and composed of excellent marksmen, forms an invincible reserve.

Then begins a strange spectacle. The front rank proceeds to insult the lion and even to send a few bullets into its retreat to make it decide to emerge.

"See it then, who thinks itself the bravest; it has not learned to show itself in front of men! It is not the bravest, it is not the lion, it is nothing but a cowardly thief! May God damn it!"

The lion, which sometimes can be glimpsed while being treated thus, tranquilly looks about, yawns, stretches, and appears to be unaware of everything which is taking place about it. However, some stray bullets hit it. Then it comes, magnificent with audacity and courage, to place itself in front of the thicket which held it. There is silence. The lion roars, rolls its huge eyes, draws back, crouches, rises, causes all the branches around it to snap with its body and tail.

The front rank fires a volley; the lion springs and most often falls under the fire of the second rank which has entered the intervals of the first. That moment is critical, for the lion does not stop the struggle until a bullet has struck it in the head or in the heart. It is not rare to see it continuing to fight with ten or twelve bullets through the body; the men on foot never bring it down without having some of their number killed or wounded.

The horsemen who have accompanied the men on foot have nothing to do as long as their enemy does not leave the broken ground; their role begins if, as sometimes comes to pass during the incidents of the battle, the men on foot succeed in forcing the lion onto a plateau or the plain. Then a different battle tactic is used, which also has interest and originality. Each horseman, according to his agility and boldness, launches his horse into a headlong gallop, fires on the lion as at a target from close range, wheels his horse the instant he has fired and goes farther away to reload and begin afresh.

The lion, attacked from all sides, wounded at each moment, always makes a stand, bounds forward, retreats, returns, and does not succumb until after a glorious struggle, but its defeat must end fatally, for, against Arab horses and riders, its success is impossible. It has no more than three terrible leaps; its run as a consequence lacks agility.

An ordinary horse outstrips it easily. It is necessary to have seen such a combat in order to gain an idea of it. Each horseman shouts an imprecation, words cross, the burnooses wave, the gunpowder thunders; one presses forward, dodges; the lion roars, the bullets whistle, it is truly moving.

Despite that tumult, accidents are very rare. The hunters have scarcely anything to fear other than a fall, which would throw them under the claws of the lion or, a more frequent mishap, a friendly but badly aimed bullet.

Now there has been made known the most picturesque, the most warlike form the hunting of the lion can assume. That hunting is done, moreover, by methods which, perhaps, have something even surer and, furthermore, more promptly efficacious about them.

The Arabs have noted that on the day after it has killed and eaten some animal the lion, under the sway of a difficult digestion, remains in its retreat, tired, sleepy, incapable of moving about. When a spot, ordinarily troubled by roars, remains silent for an entire night, it can be imagined that the redoubtable guest who inhabits it is plunged into that state of torpor. Then a courageous, dedicated man goes, by following its trail, as far as the massif where the monster keeps itself, aims, and kills it instantly by lodging a bullet between the eyes. Kaddour-ben-Mohammed, of the Oulad-Messelem faction of the Ounougha, is said to have killed many lions in that manner.

Various kinds of ambuscades are also employed against the lion. Sometimes the Arabs make a pit on the route to its retreat which they cover with a thin layer of planks. The weight of the animal breaks that thin layer and it finds itself caught in the trap. Sometimes a pit is dug near a carcass, and covered with strong planks arranged so that there is left only the opening necessary for a rifle barrel to pass through. It is in that pit, called a *melebda*, that the hunter lies in wait. At the moment the lion approaches the carcass, the hunter takes careful aim and fires. Often the lion, if it has not been hit, springs on the *melebda*, claws the planks apart and devours the hunter behind his wrecked rampart. Again, some men undertake an adventurous and heroic hunt, recalling chivalresque prowess, against the lion. Here is how, as he recounted it himself, Si Mohammed-ben-Esnoussi, a man of renowned veracity, who lived in the Djebel-Gueroul, close to Tiaret, undertook it. "I rode a good horse" (it is Mohammed himself speaking) "and I arrived at the forest during a night when the moon shone. I was a good marksman then, my bullet never fell to the earth. I started shouting a number of times '*Ataïah!*' The lion emerged and started toward the spot from which the shout came and I fired at it immediately. Often one lair would contain many lions which all emerged together. If one of those beasts approached me from behind I turned my head and sighted over my horse's croup; then, out of fear of having missed, I departed at a gallop. If I were attacked from the front, I turned my horse and began the same maneuver."

The people of the district affirm that the number of lions killed by Si Mohammed-ben-Esnoussi came close to one hundred. That intrepid hunter was still living in the year A.H. 1235 (A.D. 1836). When I saw him he had lost his sight. May he enjoy God's mercy!

A hunt even more dangerous than that directed against the lion itself is the hunt for one of its young. Yet men can always be found to attempt that dangerous undertaking. Every day the lion and lioness leave their den toward three or four o'clock in the afternoon to go far away to make a reconnaissance, for the purpose, no doubt, of procuring food for their family. They can be seen on a height examining the *douars*, the smoke arising from them, the placement of the flocks. They go away after having uttered a few horrible roars which are priceless warnings for the surrounding villages.

It is during that absence that it is necessary to slip in skillfully to the young and carry them off, being careful to muzzle them tightly, for their cries could not fail to attract a father and mother who would never grant pardon. After a coup of that nature an entire district should redouble its vigilance. For seven or eight days there are frantic searches and atrocious roars. The lion becomes terrible; it is not necessary then that eye should meet eye.

The flesh of the lion, although it is sometimes eaten, is not good. Its skin, however, is a priceless gift; it is given but to sultans, illustrious chieftains, or to the Marabouts and the *zaouïas*. The Arabs believe that it is well to sleep on a lion's skin; in that way, demons are made to keep their distance, bad luck is exorcised, and one is preserved from

certain maladies. The lion's claws, mounted in silver, become orna-
ments for the women; the skin of its forehead is a talisman which certain men place on their heads to keep audacity and energy in their
brains. To sum up, the hunting of the lion is held in great honor in
Arab lands. Every encounter with a lion could have as an adage: "Kill
or be killed."

He who kills it, eats it, says the proverb, and he who does not kill
it is himself eaten. Also there is applied to a man who has killed a
lion this laconic and virile eulogy; it is said of him: "That man there.
That is he (*Hadak houa*)."

A popular belief demonstrates the greatness of the role which the
lion plays in Arab lives and imaginations. When the lion roars, the
people assert that there can easily be distinguished these words: "*Ahna
ou ben el mera* (I and the son of woman)." Or, as it twice repeats
ben el mera and does not say *ahna* but once, it is concluded that it does
not recognize above it any but the son of woman.

12

THE CAMEL

How could we not love the camel?[1]
It bears us from the land of oppression to that of liberty.

The Prophet has said, "The goods of this world, until the Day of Final
Judgment, are bound to the forelocks of your horses. Sheep are a bene-
diction. And the Almighty, upon making animals, has not created
anything preferable to the camel."

The camel is the ship of the desert. God has said, "You can load
merchandise on ships and on the camel."

And, because in the desert there is little water and there are great
distances to traverse, the Almighty has given camels the power to
withstand thirst easily. In winter they seldom drink.

The Prophet has often made the following recommendations,
"Never pursue with coarse purposes either the camel or the wind; the
first is a blessing for men; the second is an emanation from the soul of
God."

Camels are the most extraordinary of all animals and yet they are
not seen to be more submissive because of their familiarity with man.
Their habit of docility is such that a camel has been seen to follow a

[1] I am not unaware that that term is not the one science gives to that animal,
which is the dromedary. If I have retained the term "camel," it is because it is the
only one which is in use in Algeria. Moreover the Arab word *djemel* is applied
just as well to the camel as to the dromedary.

rat which, upon gnawing it, tugged on a thong smeared with butter with which the camel had been tied. It is God Who has willed it thus.

Without drawing immediate conclusions from all those [foregoing] aphorisms, it can already be seen that the camel is the most useful animal created by God for the needs of the Arabs.

At first we shall show what the camel is from its birth to its death. We shall also accept what the Arabs say about the animal in their speech, now poetic and now trivial. What does it matter, if what they say can set one on the path to new or useful details?

A troop of one hundred camels is called an *ybeul* and it is not unusual for wealthy Arabs to own two or three *ybeuls*, that is to say, from two to three hundred camels. An *ybeul* contains thirty-five or forty she-camels (*naga*) and two males destined for stud (*faâl*). The other males are remorselessly gelded.

The *faâl* are never used as beasts of burden. They are chosen, insofar as possible, with a solid coat, all black, all bay, or all gray; [with] the eyes large and black; good height, good legs, a strong hump, a long neck, a broad breast with the *kuerkuera* (sternum) very prominent; the greatest of care is taken of them. Before use is made of them [for stud] it is necessary that they have proved on numerous journeys their strength, their vigor, and, above all, their sobriety. The latter trait is indispensable. Never would a stud be made of a camel that could not endure hunger, something which can be recognized when it stops, has to be prodded along the way, and sweats a great deal. It is then called *nezaf*. It is also unusual that a camel be devoted to stud before the age of five or six years; it is necessary for it to have acquired its full strength.

The *faâl* comes into rut in the second month of winter. It then causes an extraordinary sound to be heard. It is said: "the *faâl ihydje*." The *faâl* does not resemble in any way the males of other animals. It drools, it spumes, it bugles, a sort of bladder of flesh extrudes from its mouth, it no longer wants to eat, it loses its belly, it is often in erection, and as it always stales to the rear, it frequently pisses on its tail.

The *faâl* in rut becomes so vicious that only its master or its driver can approach it and if, by chance, despite the minute precautions which are taken, it encounters another *faâl*, it gnashes its teeth and unleashes a furious attack on it. If there is no success in separating them by blows with clubs, they inflict frightful wounds on each other. It is not unusual to see one of them die with the cervical or vertebral column broken. The *faâl* is left in that state [of rut] for five or six days, care being taken to hobble it to avoid accidents. Then, when it is well prepared, the she-camels are brought to it, but, not to tax it, it is given only one each day. The she-camel is chosen from among those which are most advanced in season and is called *mysseur*. The she-camel is taken to the *faâl*, its hobbles are removed, it throws itself on her, puts its neck over hers, and forces her to couch, as when camels are loaded. The *faâl* then spreads its entire length along the female's back, its eyes gleam with an extraordinary light, spume emerges from its mouth, and it remains for a long time in that position. The act of copulation over, it rises; the she-camel rises also. The *faâl's* hobbles are replaced.

The *faâl,* say the Arabs, is truly noble. They find proof of that in the fact that it vigorously repudiates any alliance with its dam or sister. [In order] to deceive a camel, someone presented its dam to it, covered with woolen cloths from head to feet, but the trick did not succeed. After having approached, the camel recognized her; then it rent itself with its teeth and, furious, threw itself upon the perpetrator of the deception and killed him! That tale, widely spread throughout the desert, proves, I believe, that in breeding all consanguinity is everywhere mercilessly repudiated.

A *faâl* does not cover more than forty to fifty she-camels in a season. If it is given too many, there is a risk of ruining it. Toward the middle of the spring its rut (*ydjefeur*) is over and then it starts eating with an incredible voracity to recoup its losses and restore itself after its long abstinence.

When a herd [of camels] is at pasture the she-camels scatter to right and left and the *faâl* that is in rut, displaying a great jealousy, watches all of them. If one of them goes close to one of the males destined to carry burdens only, which are called *aâzara* (servants), the *faâl* throws itself on her, bites, strikes, and calls her to order. It is exactly like a rooster with its hens. The vigorous *faâl* acquires such an ascendency over all the other camels in the herd that those that are not noble, although in the midst of she-camels in season, do not dare to approach them and, say the Arabs, do not even dare to look at them. If one seeks to usurp the rights reserved exclusively for the *faâl*, it immediately feels the wrath of the latter and receives the punishment for its audacity. It is most certainly another matter when two *faâl* happen to meet. However, it has been noted that one of the two always recognizes the power of the other and gives way.

The she-camel which has been served conceives such a love for the *faâl* that she never wants to leave it. That singular attachment is much stronger among the young females than among the old ones. The she-camel gestates for twelve months. When she has given birth she is called *legha* or *aâchera*. The Arabs take care of her, they spare her greatly; it is only the poor who load her as usual, and even they are careful not to do so at least one month before she gives birth. Abortions are common. A shepherd who, through his own fault, has allowed a she-camel to abort or a camel to do itself some injury, is obliged to pay its price. The female never bears more than one youngster in a year. Often she is given to the male after giving birth and, if she "sticks," the little one already born takes the name of *ould aâchar*. Often, however, it is necessary to wait until the following winter to give her to the male; it depends upon her condition. A she-camel who receives the male after giving birth and conceives is highly esteemed; she is a source of wealth and it is said of her: "*Naga kuessab kher min fareus saadi* (A fertile she-camel is worth more than a joyous [because of booty] horseman)."

As soon as the she-camel has given birth she is carefully covered from the hump to the tail. Her little one takes the name of *haouar*. It is covered also, completely, but with the [added] precaution of opening a slit in the covering for the hump to come through, which will allow it to grow straight and not crooked. The female no longer goes out to graze. For seven or eight days she is made to couch near the tent under which her little one is sheltered because of the cold. It is taught to nurse in this fashion: a man greases his finger with warm butter and introduces it into its mouth. The little one starts sucking; it is then carried over and placed under its mother. At the end of a few lessons it suckles and afterward continues alone.

To prevent accidents which could occur during the first few days after birth, there are Arabs who take care of the young to the extent of placing it in a sack, *gherara* (a sack for carrying bundles). It is enveloped as far as the neck, with only the head protruding, and is placed thus beside its mother. The she-camel is very fond of her young. However, when it is presented [for her] to nurse, the younger the she-camel is, the more precautions are necessary. At the end of seven or eight days the she-camel, with her baby, can be sent out to pasture. Later the baby learns by itself to couch. When it sees its dam doing it, it follows her example.

The baby camel nurses during the spring and summer. The following autumn and winter it can nurse for but a short while in the morning and in the evening. Then milking the she-camel for the needs of the tent is begun. To prevent the baby from nursing during the last month a net is placed over the mother's udder and tied over her loins. That net is called *chemâl*. Lastly, when it is desired to wean the young camel completely, it is placed in another tent or in another herd. At the end of twenty or twenty-five days it forgets its dam and the milk of the latter dries up.

The little one, the weanling (*mekhreloul*) goes to graze with the other camels; it is not yet shorn; it is a year old. At two years of age it is called *ould el boun*; it is first shorn. At three years of age it is called *djedâa*; it is shorn, and the poor, who do not have time to wait, begin to load it lightly. At four years of age it is called *heug*; it can be loaded by everyone, rich or poor. At five years of age, it is called *rebâa* or *el goôud*; it is a made camel. The female is called *bekra*. At six years of age it is definitively called *djemel*; it can be made into a *faâl*.

She-camels are more esteemed than the males; that can be understood. Those that are barren are called *ferouga*.

Concerning the Care Camels Require

The Arabs of the Sahara assert that [they can tell] the age of a camel very well by its teeth. They say that it is long lived. They cannot give figures but indicate it in this manner: a camel is born on the same day as a baby boy. That camel will be old when the boy has already made himself known for his bravery in combat. That would suppose eighteen to twenty years.

Camels require a great deal of care and great experience in their management. When possible the male camels are taken to graze apart from the females.

Beginning on the fifteenth day of April the camels are no longer sent to pasture until after midday because it has been noted that before that hour the plants are covered with dew (*neda*) which would become a source of fatal maladies. Care is also taken not to allow the camels to eat in the *douars* the grass left over in the morning from the rations given the horses during the night. These precautions should be taken for a month and a half or two months, until there is no longer any dew. During the entire winter, from the end of autumn to the first month of spring, the camels may be allowed to eat salt bushes, it will do them good; but from the beginning of April until the end of May they should be allowed to do so for but five or six days.

Here are the names of the plants and shrubs on which camels ordinarily feed. Many are known, others are not.

CAMEL FODDER: SHRUBS

El adjerem

El alned

El arfedj (*arboris spinosae* species)

El belbal

El bethom (*terebinthus*)

Chiehh

El dereuf

El djad

El djefen (*radix vitis*)

El djelàb

Ech-chbrag (*planta rubros fructus habens et rubrum lignum quocum sanguis occisorum comparatur*)

Ed-djedar (*nomen herbae crescentis in arenis*)

Ed-doum

En-nagad (*anthemis*)

Er-ràbi

Er-reguir

Er-reteum (*genista frutex*)

Es-sad (*cyperus*)

Es-saliân (*herbae seu oleris* species)

Es-sedra (*ziziphus lotus*)

Es-sefar (*herbae spinosae*)

Et-tafegh

Et-tharf (*tamarix*)

Ez-zit (*oleum olivarum*)

El ferou

El fil

El ghàres

El gueteum

El guethof (*Atriplex halimus*)

Guezahh (*seminis cepae*)

El hadj (*colocynthis*)

El igthàn

El karteum

El kelokh

El khodar

El khorchef (wild artichokes)
El koubar
El kuertem
El kuesob
Larth
Lazal
El meker (*herniara*)
El merakh (*cynanchum viminale*)
El nasi (*cardui* species)

El nedjil
El oussera
Teskir (*hyoscyamus*)
Tiguentcuse
El yanthite
Yathithar
El zateur
Zeboudje (wild olives)

CAMEL FODDER: PLANTS (*el aâcheub*)

El aâkuif
El aarirb (scabiosa)
El âdeme (*zizamia*)
El adjerem
Afli
El alfa
Azbiân
El âzir
El bageul (*olus, speciatim portu-laca*)
El beajiq
Ben-naamàn (field poppy)
El bibache
El bine
Bou-kharis
Bou-nagar
El chegaâ
Chiehh
El derine (*stipa barbata*)
Deubàl
Dil-el-fàr (literally, rat's tail)
El djemir (*ficus sycomorus*)
Drâa
Ech-cheliath
Ech-cherirah
Ed-delnef
Ed-demrâne

En-nedjem (*nomen plantae* [*sic*] in the dictionary)
En-neguig
En-netil
Er-reguigue
Er-reumt
Es-sambari
Es-seleuse (*cardui* species)
Es-senagh
Es-sigue
Et tàlem
Ez-zafzàf (*ziziphum*)
Ez-zagza
El garthoufa (*olus*)
El ghebir (*ruellia guttata*)
El guehouân (*anthemis*)
El guelgelàne (*dolichos cuneifolius*)
El guiz
Hamimeuch
El hamma
El haref
El harmel (*pegamen harmala*)
El heulm (*herba arnoglossa albicans foliis et lanuginosa*)
El hhar
El karneb (brassica)
El kerat

El kerkaz
El khaufeur
El khebir (*malva*)
El khemoun (cuminum)
El kheud
El ksibeur
El kuikoute
Ledena
Lella
Lezoul
El mâk
El mechith (*polypodium crenatum*)
El medjil

El melahh
El metnân
El mourar (species *arboris scu plantae amara* [*sic*])
El mrar (*absynthum*)
El Ouchàm (*plantae germen*)
Oudene-en-nadja (literally, ewe's ear)
El reguime (*malva*)
Sag-el-gherabe (crowsfoot)
Sor
Ticheret

The camels should be watered every three days in summer and autumn. In winter they drink little, unless it is hot, and, in the latter event, every eight or ten days. At the beginning of spring they do not drink, at the end they drink every day; that depends upon the quantity of pasture and on its more (or less) aqueous quality.

It is also necessary from April until the autumn that the camels not be watered at ponds (*ghedir*); the stagnant waters they contain cause such grave maladies as *el ghedda* and *el téhan*, which limpid water would prevent.

Customary Camel Medicine

Gelding. The wealthy have castrated among their herds the camels destined for journeys and that is [done] in order to get rid of the nuisance they cause when they are in rut. The gelding is ordinarily done with a sickle reddened in the fire. The testicle is made to emerge by a line of fire on the skin, then the suspensory ligament is cut by another line of fire. That operation, which is generally successful, is not, however, without some danger. It should not be performed in either cold weather or the season of great heat. The gelded camel is called a *zouzâl*.

Tarring. Each year, after the camel shearing, the camels, large and small, are tarred. They are tarred twice during the spring and once during the summer. That operation has as its object preserving them from the scab. If it is not done, the Arabs say, a third of the troop will die, for it [the scab] has then (in the springtime) done its work in the blood and skin.

When the chieftain of a tent wants to tar his camels, all his neighbors, at his invitation, come to help him. The camels are made to couch, each animal's lower lip has a cord twisted around it [a twitch], and they are daubed from head to foot. That operation is concluded in a day.

The tar is liquid, it is mixed with *leben* (sour milk). It is made in almost all the *kuesours* (villages) of the desert; that which is made from *taga* is worth more than that which comes from the *aârare*. A goatskin of tar (about twenty-five liters), is worth one Spanish *douro* (5 fr. 40 to 5 fr. 60).

Purging. It is at shearing and tarring time that the camels are ordinarily purged. A pound of rancid butter (*deheun*) is boiled in a pot, mixed with three or four eggs, then wool with yolk on it is added. The wool is removed, the camel is made to swallow the potion, and thus a violent purge is obtained.

Diseases of the Camel

The principal diseases of the camel are: *el ghedda*, an internal malady; *el bou chelalle*, an internal malady and pissing of blood; *el téhan*, also an internal malady; *el djereub*, scab; and galls on the withers. It is also said that should the camel eat grass on which blood has been spilled it will surely die. It is, moreover, generally accepted that if a woman has relations with her lover in the midst of a herd of camels, during the night, those camels will all fall ill and part of them will die. It is what is called *el nedjeuss*.

El debabe. The *debabe* are very large flies which appear at the end of April and in the month of May. When they attach themselves to the animals they give them stings which are so bloody, so painful, that they become like mad creatures and sometimes contract fatal diseases. The camels greatly fear the *debabe*; therefore all imaginable precautions are taken to protect them from the flies. Here is the most efficacious: the tribe brings together all its *douars* in order to have a great number of animals in a small space, which divides the *debabe* endlessly and makes them less dangerous. This means of protection is called *tedjenâa*.

If by chance a journey is made during the *debabe* season there is no means of getting rid of them other than by driving them off with the smoke of small fires lighted around the camels. The *debabe* are unknown beyond Laghouat and the [country of the] Oulad-Sidi-Chikh.

Mayâref chi lel Behaire Et-tob-Ghèr elli rebah

(No one knows the medicine of camels but he who has bred some).

The Usefulness of the Camel; the Benefit Derived from It

It is toward the end of April when the camels are shorn. The shearing is undertaken in the following way: The camels are couched and then the Negresses and drovers start shearing with very sharp knives, while a woman comes along behind them to gather the hair (*el oubeur*), which she puts into sacks. That operation requires a lot of time. *El oubeur* serves for making tent material, camel's-hair cords, sacks called *gherara*, blankets for horses (*djellale*). Almost always *el oubeur* is mixed with ordinary wool.

The usual burden of a camel is two *tellis* of wheat (about five hundred pounds). If its driver does not urge it, the camel can travel from the break of day until the setting of the sun, on the condition, furthermore, that it is able, by stretching its neck to right and left along the way, to browse on the grass and shrubs within its reach. The camel in that manner can travel close to forty-five miles a day, but it is necessary, every five days, to give it a day of rest.

In the desert camels are hired not at so much per day, but at so much per journey to go and return, according to the distance. For example, from El Biod of the Oulad-Sidi-Chikh to the Beni-Mzab (about two hundred miles) [it costs] two or three *douros*, and from the same point to Timimoun, six or seven.

The sage Monalef has written somewhere that our lord Jacob had prohibited the eating of the flesh of the camel, because upon having tasted it, he felt himself to be transported with unknown desires for women.

Ben-Zoubir said, "The flesh of the camel augments the vigor of man; its urine sobers the drunken; its hair, reduced to ashes, stops hemorrhages; and its fleas (*guerade*) placed on a lover's clothing will take away his desire."

However it may be, the Arabs eat the flesh of the camel. It is not bled, however, except when it has a broken leg or when it is ill; it is very unusual to see a healthy camel slaughtered. The flesh is also salted; it is dried in the sun and kept as a provision for journeys. That dried flesh is called *khreléa*.

The love, the veneration, which the Arabs of the Sahara have for the camel can be understood. "How," they say, "could we not love the camels? *Alive*, they carry us—us, our women, our children, our baggage, and our provisions—from the land of oppression to that of liberty. The weight with which they can be burdened is enormous; the distances they cover are considerable. It is enough to say that they favor commercial relations and are useful in war. Thanks to them we can, whenever we please, change camp grounds to find new pastures or flee from our enemies. We drink the milk of the she-camels, which is, moreover, priceless in the preparation of food to mitigate the pernicious effects of the date.

"*Dead*, their flesh is eaten everywhere with pleasure; everywhere the hump (*deroua*) is sought after as a delicious dish. Their hide serves to make footgear. Soaked and then sewn over a saddletree it gives, without the aid of one nail, of one peg, a solidity capable of great resistance. Lastly [the camels'] sobriety and resistance to thirst and heat permit of their being kept by the poor as well as the rich. They are truly God's blessing. He has said:

> " '*El kheïl lel bela,*
> *El begeur lel fekeur*
> *El ybeul lel khela*
>
> (Horses for combat,
> Oxen for poverty
> Camels for the desert).' "

Now then, *could the camel be acclimated to France?* That is the question which I felt I should pose myself as the conclusion of all the foregoing. To resolve it (that question) I have just, moreover, consulted a highly intelligent Arab, at this moment on a trip to Paris. He is named Abd-el-Kader-ben Khatir and he belongs to a considerable tribe of the province of Oran; to the tribe of the Zmélas.

Here is how he answered me, "I believe that the acclimatization of the camel to France would be very difficult. The camel loves hot and sandy lands. It flees from humid and marshy climes. The camel desires space; your properties seem to me to be well marked off. That would be to kill the camel by enclosing it.

"France would not appear to me to possess the salty shrubs and the plants which the camel eats in Africa. But, even supposing that she did have them, could the camel, when traveling, amuse itself by nibbling everywhere to the right and left of the road? Obviously not, your laws and the divisions of your lands would oppose it in an invincible manner. Would your fodders successfully replace the varied nourishment which the camel encounters among us? I do not believe so.

"And, lastly, the camel fears the cold. *The earth is hot in Algeria*; the cold there does not last. In Algeria each station of the year is of three months' duration. In France the weather does not settle and the seasons there are frequently inverted."

13

THE KHEBECH SHEEP

She sees like the owl and
travels like the tortoise.

Cattle are not raised in the Sahara. Why? Because water is scarce, pasture is not very abundant, the terrain is rocky, and migrations from one place to another are very frequent. But, if the desert is not favorable for the development of the bovine species, it is, on the other hand, the true fatherland of the sheep. There it finds all the salty shrubs of which we have spoken with regard to the camel, as well as a host of other odoriferous and nutritive plants known under the generic term of *el aâcheub*.

The sheep are watered from pools formed by rainfall or from troughs, built at the sides of wells and maintained with particular care. These wells are, more often than not, surrounded by low masonry copings and placed under shelter from the sands. Sheep can withstand thirst. They are watered, in the spring, every five or six days; in the summer, every two days; in autumn, every three days, and in winter, every four days. The use of small puddles of water scattered about on the ground is banned to them during the great heat of summer. It has been noted that at that time of year all stagnant water, heated by the sun, becomes very harmful to the sheep.

When there has been a drought during the first two months of spring but the third month has been so rainy that the grass has sprung up in abundance, that grass is called *khelfa* (replacement). The sheep, as if to compensate for their long abstinence, eat it with avidity, but it always causes an illness called *el ghoche* (betrayal). This does not declare itself until the summer heat. Then the head and lower portions of the jaws swell considerably, the animal coughs a great deal, very often it dies. According to the Arabs a rainy autumn which brings the new spring grass early in the desert considerably diminishes the pernicious effects of *el ghoche*.

The ewes are very fertile. They usually lamb twice a year, at the beginning of autumn and the beginning of spring.

Large tribes possess from two to three hundred thousand sheep. Those sheep are divided, for supervision, into flocks of four hundred head which are called *ghrelem* or *aâssa* (cane). Wealthy people have from fifteen to twenty *ghrelem*, the poorest a half-*ghrelem*, a quarter of a *ghrelem*. In a *ghrelem* there should be some thirty rams and a certain number of wethers. The latter, always fatter than the others, are destined for trade or for the demands of hospitality.

In the Sahara there is a breed of sheep which gives magnificent wool, very fine, but not very long.[1] It is from that wool that the luxury cloths are woven. The heads of the sheep are almost red. The ewes also give a great quantity of milk; unfortunately no pains are taken in breeding them. The most esteemed ewes of that breed are those of which it is said:

> *Techouf, choufel el hama*
> *Ou temchy, mechit el haytama.*
>
> (She sees like the owl
> And travels like the tortoise.)

The wool descends as far as the hooves and covers the head in such a way that literally only the eyes can be seen. In the Sahara and in the *kuesours* the fleece (*zedja*) of one sheep is worth no more than one *boudjou*. Taken to the Tell and to the coast it increases in price.[2]

Some sheep are found which do not have any horns; they are called

---

[1] This is the merino. [Translator's note]
[2] The Europeans today are carrying on a large wool trade in the Sahara.

fertass (bald). To the contrary some are seen that have four. They are designated under the name of *el kuerboube*. Lastly others have curved horns and are known as *el kher-ouby*.

The Arabs do not take any care of their sheep. They do not have either folds to shelter them from the inclemencies of the season or stores of fodder to save them from starvation. Thus, during bad years, they frequently lose half their flocks. When they are reproached for that negligence, or when it is desired to give them advice, they simply reply, "However wise that may be, it is the blessing of God [*kher-eurby*]. He shall do what He wills. Our ewes give us two lambs a year. Next year our losses will be recouped."[3]

The Arabs attribute to the sheep the following speech:

> (*Nehheb el id chedida*
> *Ou souag el baâida*
> *Ou dar djedida*)

I want a closed hand (that is to say, I want to belong to a miser who will not sell me or have me slaughtered to regale his guests) ;

Distant markets (when they are near to my master for some reason or other, I will be sold, I will be slaughtered) ;

A new lodging each day (that is to say, new and more abundant pastures).

Sheep are the fortune of the children of the desert. They call them *el metmir rahala* (ambulatory storehouses) and say of them:

Their wool serves for making our tents, our rugs, our garments, our blankets for the horses, our sacks for bundles, our nose bags, our camel saddles, our cords, and our cushions. What exceeds our needs we sell in the *kuesours* or in the Tell when, after the harvest, we go there to buy grain.

Their flesh we eat and cause to be eaten by God's invited. Dried in the sun, it is preserved and serves us on our travels (*khreléa*).

Their milk is very useful for our families, be it as a beverage, be it as a food. We make *leben* or *chenine* (sour milk) from it and what is left over we give to our horses. We make butter from it, furthermore, which is

---

[3] However, for some time now there has been some success in having more pains taken with the breeding of sheep among certain tribes. Among them the sheep were sheared with knives or with sickles. Now it is done with shears which is some progress, at least.

used in the preparation of our food, or we trade it in the *kuesours* for dates.

Their fleece we make cushions (*mezoueud*) from and buckets (*delou*) for drawing water from a well. We decorate the *aâtatouche* (a type of chair placed on camels) of our women with it, or we prepare it for our footgear.

We have no need to till, to sow, to harvest, to thresh, to tire ourselves, in a word, like lowly slaves or the wretched inhabitants of the Tell. No. We are independent; we pray, we trade, we hunt, we travel, and, if the need were to make itself felt of procuring for ourselves that which among others is not obtained but by sweat and toil, we [would] sell some sheep and immediately procure weapons, horses, women, jewels, garments— everything which could please us or enhance our existence.

The master of some sheep has no need to labor and never lacks anything. God has willed it thus.

14

GENERALITIES CONCERNING THE DESERT

Among us the soul can always
dominate the belly.

Even upon putting aside all the amplifications which are prohibited to
me by the limits of my subject, it is, it seems to me, necessary to study
in the horseman of the Sahara another facet than that of hunter and
warrior. After having noted piece by piece his equipment for hunting
and war, his armor of a chevalier, if I may speak thus, I wish to give
a glimpse of the man, to make known the other objects with which he
surrounds himself; the motives under the influence of which he acts,
his customs, habits, and prejudices.

Less specialized than the other parts of this book, this chapter will
be more penetrating than the two works of which it is, in a way, the
complement: *Le Sahara Algérien* and *Le Grand Désert*.

In the studies which have occupied me up to the present, one thing
has struck me, above all, and that is the analogy of the life of the desert
to the life of the Middle Ages; it is the resemblance which exists between the horseman of the Sahara and the chevalier of our legends,
romances, and chronicles. The observation of accessory characteristics
which I wish to sketch rapidly will perhaps make that analogy even
more real; that resemblance even more striking.

By "horseman of the Sahara" I do not mean to designate the inhabi-

"Zaouïa, a religious establishment . . . contains the tombs of its founders." (From Élisée Reclus, *Africa*.)

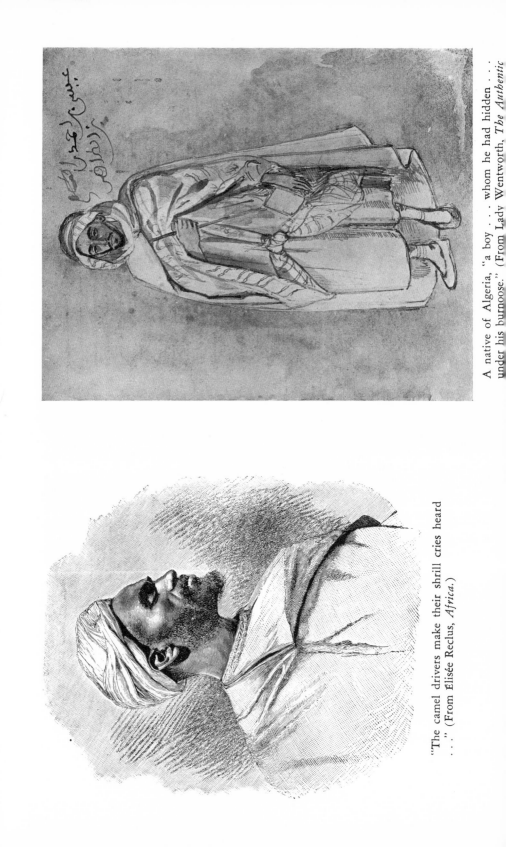

A native of Algeria, "a boy . . . whom he had hidden . . . under his burnoose." (From Lady Wentworth, *The Authentic*

"The camel drivers make their shrill cries heard . . ." (From Élisée Reclus, *Africa*.)

". . . like the cloud . . . which covers a gorge." (From Élisée Reclus, *Africa*.)

". . . when the convoy halts on a new camping ground, free from all impurity." (From Élisée Reclus, *Africa*.)

"... the lances of the Tuaregs, *those veiled brigands* of the desert ..." (From Élisée Reclus, *Africa*.)

"The palm of the land of the Beni-Mzab." (From Élisée Reclus, *Africa*.)

"... preliminary words on [the merits of] coffee without sugar." (From Élisée Reclus, *Africa*.)

" . . . *kuerraba*, lockets in which the women put benzoin or *zebeud*." (From Élisée Reclus, *Africa*.)

"It is the *chelil* of the horse Borak." (From Lady Wentworth, *Thoroughbred Racing Stock*.)

"Distant markets. (When they are close . . . I will be sold, I will be slaughtered.)" (From Élisée Reclus, *Africa*.)

Targui type, showing native dress." (From
sée Reclus, *Africa.*)

"For them the cottonstuffs, the woolen garments." (From Élisée Reclus, *Africa.*)

"How many gallant horsemen have died for
her on fighting!" (From Élisée Reclus, *Africa.*)

he owner . . . would not exchange it for a
gress." (From Élisée Reclus, *Africa.*)

"The age of the animal . . . by the rin
on its horns . . ." (From Lady Wen
worth, *Thoroughbred Racing Stock.*)

"Softly, softly," speak the stirrups the
. . ." (From Lady Wentworth, *The A.
thentic Arabian Horse.*)

"He is like the ostrich. He goes where he sees the
lightning flash." (From Lady Wentworth, *The
Authentic Arabian Horse.*)

"On our haouadjej lie virgins .
(From Major-General W. Twee
C.S.I., *The Arabian Horse: His Cou
and People.*)

tant of the *kuesours* (the townsman). The nomads deride the latter as
much as [they do] the inhabitant of the Tell and heap mocking epi-
thets on him. Fattened as he is by sedentary habits and the merchant
life, they call him "the father of the belly, the grocer, the pepper merchant, *sekakri*." That poultry raiser, that shopkeeper resembles the
bourgeois of any land, of any age. He is, basically, the common man,
the villein of the Middle Ages. He is the Moor, the townsman of Algiers; [he has] the same placid, apathetic, and cunning countenance.

I mean to speak of the lord of the tent, of him who never stays more
than fifteen or twenty days [in the same place] without moving on—
the true nomad, he who does not go to the wearisome Tell but once a
year to buy grain. My horseman, my hunter, my warrior is that man
with a lean and muscular build, face burned by the sun, well-propor-
tioned limbs, large rather than small, always making good use of the
advantage of height, of that "lion's skin on a cow's frame (*djeld sebaa
ala dohor el beugra*)," when he has not added to it skill, agility,
health, vigor, and, above all, courage. Though he esteems courage, he
pities and does not disdain or ever insult those who lack "liver" (*keubda*). It is not their fault God has so disposed matters. He is of an
extreme abstemiousness but, yielding to circumstance he does not neglect an opportunity to eat well and heartily. His daily food is simple
and little varied, but he understands how to regale his guests worthily,
when it is necessary. When *el ouadâa* comes, a saint's feast day of a
tribe, of a *douar*, where his friends are gathered, he would never prof-
fer them the insult of not attending. And, were it one hundred or more
miles away, it would be necessary that he go and satiate his belly. Moreover, his friends know that he is ever ready to render them a similar
service; that they are not dealing with one of those mercantile misers
of the towns whose entire effort at hospitality goes only as far as the
offer of four square feet to sit on, a pipe of tobacco, and a cup of coffee without sugar, or sugared after carefully weighed preliminary
words on [the merits of] coffee without sugar.

Everything about the Arab concurs with the power manifest in the
outdoor life. Sinewy, toughened, abstemious—although occasionally
with a great appetite—he has a sure and piercing eye. He vaunts his
ability to distinguish a man from a woman at several miles; at twenty

miles, a herd of camels from a flock of sheep. Is that boasting? Certainly not. The extent and keenness of his eyesight, could they not come to him, as to our mariners, from the lifelong habit of gazing into a distance of immense and barren spaces? Then, too, accustomed to objects and scenes which, ever the same, surround him within a certain radius, it would be strange if he could not recognize them in any weather. Notwithstanding, diseases of the eyes are frequent.[1] The glare of the sun, the dust, sweat, cause a host of accidents, white spots on the cornea and ophthalmias, for instance. The blind and the one-eyed are numerous in many localities of the desert, among the Beni-Mzab, at El Ghrassoul, at Ouargla, and at Gourara.

The man of the desert has, in his childhood and even in his young manhood, beautiful teeth, white and even, but dates, as a customary and almost exclusive diet, ruin them as he grows older. When a tooth is completely rotten it is to the armorers and farriers that he must resort. They are the ones in a position to martyrize the patient, to break his jaw with a pair of pliers and to remove the gum at the same time as the sore tooth.

The true great lord, the important chieftain, rarely leaves the saddle and scarcely ever walks. He wears boots (*temag*) and slippers; but the common man is an indefatigable walker; he covers incredible distances in one day. His ordinary walk is what we call the gymnastic pace. He himself calls it the dogtrot. Generally on even ground he removes his footgear, when he has any, to travel faster and more comfortably and also not to wear it out. As a consequence they [the walkers] all have the feet of ancient statues—wide, well and firmly planted, the big toe not jutting out. They do not know what corns are, and more than once a Christian who introduced himself into a caravan found himself expelled, betrayed by that infallible sign. The soles of their feet acquire such a toughness that sand or rocks no longer injure them; a thorn sometimes penetrates a few inches without their noticing it.

Nonetheless, in the desert proper, during the great heat of summer

---

[1] I have, in a preceding book, *Le Grand Désert,* indicated the use the Arabs make of *koheul* (sulphur of antimony). It is, together with bloodlettings from the feet and head, the only curative means employed for diseases of the eyes.

the sand is so burning that it is impossible to travel barefooted; [it burns] to such an extent that it is necessary to shoe the horses lest their hooves become sore and in bad condition. Fear of the bite of the *lefâ* (carpet viper),[2] a viper which kills, also makes it necessary to wear boots coming up above the ankle bone.

The most common ailments of the feet are the cracks (*cheggag*), which are cured by smearing the affected part with grease and cauterizing it with a red-hot iron instrument. Sometimes the cracks are so wide and deep that it is necessary to sew them together. The thread used is camel sinew, dried in the sun and split into filaments as fine as silk; or, sometimes, spun camel hair. All the inhabitants of the desert make use of those threads, called *el aâgueub*, to repair their saddles, bridles, wooden vessels; each of them always carries a kit, a knife, and a sewing needle.

The talent for being admirable walkers is profited from by some, for whom it becomes a profession. It produces runners—messengers—who girth themselves tightly with a running belt. Those who are called *rekass* are entrusted with urgent matters; they make in four days the run which ordinary runners make in ten. They scarcely ever stop. When they feel the need to rest they count sixty breaths and start off again at once. A *rekass* who has done sixty leagues and has received four francs thinks himself handsomely recompensed. In the desert an extraordinary courier travels night and day. He sleeps only two hours out of the twenty-four. When he lies down he ties to his foot a cord of a certain length to which he sets fire; when the cord is on the point of being consumed, the fire awakens him.

For the rest, that modest recompense [of four francs] can be understood from the moment when it is paid in minted coins. Specie is rare and it is the least considerable portion of the Arab fortune. Circulation of coins is very restricted, because of the ease with which the greatest part of the necessities of life may be acquired without buying or selling but with recourse solely to barter, and that in very few cases—far from lowers the value of minted specie.

---

2 Lefâ: carpet viper. See note six, chapter VI.

It is, perhaps, not without interest to give the approximate inventory of the fortune of a Saharian nomad. Such an inventory, it seems to me, would, better than long descriptions, be of such a nature as to enable one to comprehend the life of the desert on the spot.

I presuppose an influential family and include in its household the following:

He, himself (the chieftain)	1
His four wives	4
His four sons	4
His two daughters-in-law (two of his sons are married)	2
One child of each of his married sons	2
Four Negroes	4
Four Negresses	4
Two white menservants	2
Two white maidservants	2
Total	25

He may have had daughters, but if so, they are married; they will no longer cause him any expense.

Furnished Tents Necessary to Shelter These Persons

douros

1. A vast tent in good condition, in a word, complete, a *khreima*. In the making of that tent six lengths of woolen cloth, forty elbows long by two wide, are used. A piece of woolen cloth of that type is called *felidje*. The *felidje* is worth seven to eight *douros*, in all, about   112

2. Two Arab beds called *el guetifa* or *el ferrache*. These are carpets of shaggy wool, thirty elbows long by five wide, dyed Turkey red; they are worth twenty *douros* each; dyed, twenty-five   50

3. A carpet twelve elbows long by four wide, serving as a divider between the men's room and the women's room. That carpet, dyed scarlet, is called *tague hambeul* and is worth   16

douros

4. Six cushions, holding garments, used for sleeping; they
   are called *ousaïdes, ous aâda* and are worth two *douros*
   each   12

5. Six cushions, called *kuerabiche*, of tanned antelope hide,
   serving to hold garments and spun yarn and to rest on in
   the tent   6

6. Six lengths of wool, called *hamale el aâtatiche*. They form
   that species of chair, called *aâtatiche*, borne by camels, in
   which the women travel   12

7. Five red *haïks* to cover the *aâtatiche*   50

8. Twenty complete *gherara* (woolen sacks for carrying
   grain)   40

9. Six *hamal* (sacks lined with wool) of wheat   48

10. Twelve *hamal* of barley   60

11. Ten *gherara* (woolen sacks in which are enclosed jewels,
    garments, cottonstuffs, *filaly*, silver, gunpowder). Two
    douros each   20

12. Fifteen *guerbas* or goatskins, for holding water for the
    tent (household)   25

13. Twelve *aokha* (sheepskins or goatskins containing the
    supply of butter for the tent), four *douros* each   48

14. Four *djeloud* (sheepskins or goatskins containing hon-
    ey). Honey is expensive. It comes from the Tell. Eight
    douros the skin   32

15. Eight *hamal* of dates. Eight *douros* each   64

16. Six *tarahh*. Six morocco leather (*filaly*) skins are thus
    termed. In all, thirty-six skins at one *douro* each   36

17. A supply of gunpowder   30

18. A supply of lead   5

19. A supply of flints   4

20. Ten *mektaa* or lengths of cotton cloth called *kuettane el
    malty*, at two *douros* the *mektaa*   20

21. Two *meradjen*, cups of enameled copper, with handles,
    for drinking water or milk   2

douros

22. Two *tassa,* other vessels of copper also for drinking   2
23. Two *guessaa* or large wooden containers for making or
    serving *couscous*   4
24. Six *bakia* or wooden drinking cups, one *réal* each   2
25. One *guedra* or *tandjera,* a copper cooking pot for meat   2
26. Three *metreud,* wooden dishes for serving food to strang-
    ers   3
27. Two *fass,* mattocks, to set up the tents and cut wood   2
28. One *kadouma* (a small hatchet to work wood)   1
29. Ten *meudjeza,* species of sickles without teeth for shear-
    ing sheep   1
30. Two *rekiza,* tent poles   2
31. Lastly, an *âeuchet el zemel,* a special tent with carpets and
    cushions, for travel or for receiving strangers   30

Clothing, Five Men

32. Eleven white burnooses, of which three are for the father,
    two for each son; the burnoose is worth four *douros*   44
33. Five *haïks,* at four *douros* each   20
34. Five *habaya* or woolen shirts, at two *douros* the shirt   10
35. Five *maharema* or morocco leather belts, embroidered in
    silk, at two *douros* each   10
36. Five pairs of *belghra* or Moroccan slippers   2
37. Five *chachia* or *fessy* from Morocco   2
38. For special occasions, five *kate* or complete ensembles:
    oughrlila, vest; *cedria,* waistcoat; *seroual,* trousers; *haïk*
    in silk; a silk cord instead of a camelhide thong; burnoose
    of wool; at sixty *douros* each ensemble   300

Clothing, Six Women

39. Six *kueca* or *haïks* for women, dyed red, at ten *douros*
    each   60
40. Six pairs of *guergue* or embroidered morocco leather
    boots, at one *douro* the pair   6

douros

41. Six *hazame* or woolen belts   12
42. Six *haouly* which the women fasten to
    their heads   6
43. Six *benica* or silk head coverings   6
44. Six *aâsaba* or narrow cords with which the women fasten
    the *haouly* on the head   2
45. Six *khrolkhrale* or pairs of anklets, made of silver, at
    twenty *douros* the pair   120
46. Six *souar* or pairs of bracelets, at seven *douros* the pair   42
47. Twelve *bezima* or silver buckles the women use to fasten
    the *haïk*, at six *douros* the pair   36
48. Six *bezimat el gueursi* or throat brooches serving to hold
    the *haouly* under the chin after it has been wound around
    the head   12
49. Twelve *ounaiss* or earrings of silver-mounted coral. Each
    woman wears two pairs   24
50. Six *mekhrengua* or necklaces of coral and pieces of silver   48
51. Six *mekhrengua* or necklaces of cloves strewn with coral   5
52. Six *sensela* or silver chains, each with a pendant in the
    center called *aguereub* (the scorpion); the chain goes
    from one ear to the other   18
53. Six *kuerraba*, silver lockets which the women hang around
    their necks and in which they put benzoin or *zebeud*[3]   18
54. Eighteen *kratem* or silver rings   6
55. Six *melyaca* or bracelets of *djamous* horn. As can be not-
    ed, women in the desert do not wear gold. All their jewel-
    ry is of silver   6

Armament for Seven Men

Five master's rifles, silver-mounted, from Algiers   100
Two servants' rifles   20
Five sabers, of which two are silver-mounted   40
Five pistols, of which two are silver-mounted   35

---

3 *Zebeud:* civet musk.

douros

Armament of the Negroes

Four pistols	12
Four sabers	12

Tack and Equipment

A master's saddle	100
Four ordinary saddles	160
Two common servants' saddles	20
One master's *djebira* (saddlebag) with tigerskin	17
Four ordinary *djebira*	28
One pair of master's *temag* (boots), of morocco leather	12
Four pairs of common boots	24
One pair of master's *chabir* (spurs), silver-plated, ornamented with coral	6
Four pairs of common *chabir*	4
Five *medol* or straw hats decked with ostrich plumes	5

Horses, Beasts, Attendants

One stallion for the head of the tent	100
Four purebred mares for his sons	320
Two servants' mares	60
Six donkeys (there are few mules in the Sahara)	18
Two salukis or gazelle hounds (they are not bought)	0
Four Negroes	240
Four Negresses	200
Twenty *ghrelem* or *aâssa* (flocks of four hundred sheep each)	8,000
Four *ybal* or troops of one hundred camels each. Out of the four hundred head there are one hundred and thirty she-camels, which are more expensive than the males. I reckon them all at an average of thirty *douros* per head	12,000
Ten goats or bucks, serving only to make the sheep travel	50
Two tame gazelles (they are not bought)	0

douros

An *oukerif-el-ouhach*, the fawn of an antelope (it is
   not bought)   0
An ostrich (it is not bought)   0

Storehouses

The master of a tent of the foregoing importance should have
   stored in three or four *kuesours*:

	douros
Twelve hundred *zedja* or fleeces, at half a *boudjou* each	200
Thirty white burnooses, at three *douros* each	90
Thirty *kueca*, women's *haïks*, at two *douros* each	60
Forty *habaya*, woolen shirts, at two *douros* each	80
Forty *hamal* of dates, at seven *douros*	280
Thirty *hamal*, or camel loads, of wheat	240
Thirty *hamal* of barley	150
Four *khrabya* (enormous clay jars), filled with butter	0

Business Dealings

I estimate at six hundred *douros* the total of that which the
   master might have lent or sold to the townspeople in the
   kuesours with whom he has business dealings   600
He has in his tent six hundred *douros*   600
He has buried in a house belonging to him in a *ksar*   1,000
   (Money is not buried in the desert as [it is] in the Tell because the winter floods might betray the hiding places.)
The house in the *ksar* is guarded by a *khremass*, and contains
   his most prized effects   60

Recapitulation

Furnished tents	741
Men's and women's clothing	815
Armament	209
Tack and equipment	376
Horses, beasts, attendants	20,988
Storehouses	1,100

	douros
Business dealings	2,200
Khremass at dwelling	60
Total	26,489

[Or] be it 143,040 francs, the *douro* being worth about 5 francs, 40 centimes.

The Arab chieftain thus supplied does not work. He goes to gatherings, to the assemblies of the *djemâa*; he hunts, rides about on horseback, looks after his herds; prays. He has only political, bellicose, and religious occupations.

The poor man himself equally disdains manual labor. Nothing obligates him to [perform] it; there is no other crop but that of dates left to the people of the *kuesours*. Negroes are numerous and cost very little. These and a few white servants are sufficient for the tasks of which free men rid themselves. Some among the latter, however, repair sacks and tack [but] that is exceptional. There are also, it is true, some farriers, but in reality they are craftsmen. The privileges which they are granted, and of which I have had occasion to speak, make of them a sort of guild apart.

Those whom I have been able to call armorers are workmen who do not manufacture, but only repair, weapons. The Arabs of the desert are, in general, worse armed than those of the Tell, although their chieftains do not yield to anyone in sumptuousness and luxury. That is understandable. They have their arms brought from Tunis through Touggourt and from Morocco through the region of Gourara. The long distances to be traversed prevent those weapons from being repaired quickly, and the lack of skill of those charged with that task does not permit that those repairs be fitting. Many Saharians are, moreover, armed with lances, which they scarcely use except to pursue fugitives. Their lance is a piece of wood six feet in length with a flat, double-edged cutting blade of iron. It is usually carried obliquely.

The Arab of the Sahara is very proud of that life which, although it is exempt from the monotonous toil to which the inhabitant of the Tell is subjected, is no less active and agitated, full of variety and unforeseen events. If the beard swiftly turns white in the desert, the cause is not the heat, the weariness, the journeys, and the combats, but the sorrows, the uneasiness, the frustrations. For the first alone do not whiten "[he who] has a broad heart" knows how to resign himself and say: "God has willed it thus."

The pride [of the Arab] in his land and in his way of life goes to the extreme of disdain for the Tell and for him who inhabits it. There is no need here to recall the taunts the inhabitants of the desert and the Tell exchange, which I have already cited elsewhere. But what the man of the desert is proudest of is his independence, for in his country the land is vast and there is no sultan. The chieftain of the tribe administers and metes out justice, a not very complicated task, for crimes are few and have often been foreseen and the penalties fixed in advance.

He who steals a ewe [pays] a fine of ten *boudjous*; he who enters a tent to see his neighbor's wife pays ten ewes; he who kills pays with his life. Should he have fled, everything that belonged to him is confiscated, except for the tent, which is left to his wife and children. The fines are kept by the *djemâa* to defray [the expenses of] travelers and Marabouts and to make gifts to strangers.

Thefts committed within the tribe are severely punished; those committed in another tribe, tolerated; in an enemy tribe, encouraged.

The women do the cooking, weave carpets called *ferrache*; *tags*, rugs to make the divisions within the tent; *hamal*, *gherara*, sacks for grain; *el felidje*, cloth for making tents; *el djellale*, horse blankets; *el haouya*, camel pack-saddles; *el aâmayre*, nose bags. The burnooses, *haïks*, and *habaya* are made in the *kuesours*. The Negresses gather wood and draw water.

Wealthy, the Arab is generous. Rich or poor, he is hospitable and charitable. Rarely does he lend his horse, but it would be an insult to send it back to him. To all gifts he responds with a gift of much greater value. He is of those men who are cited as never having refused anyone. A proverb says: "He who addresses himself to the nobility never comes away empty-handed."

There is no need to speak of alms. Everyone knows that only less than the Holy War, and to the same degree as making pilgrimages, the giving of alms is the act most pleasing to God. If an Arab is in the process of eating, and a beggar passes by who cries: "*Mtâ rebi ia el moumenin* (that which belongs to God or believers)," the believer will share his repast, if there is enough for two, or he will give it all away.

A stranger presents himself at a *douar*; [if] he halts at a certain distance and speaks these words: "*dif rebi* (a guest sent by God)," the effect is magical. Whatever his condition, one hastens to him, he is tugged at, the stirrup is held for him to dismount. The servants take charge of his mount and he will have no need to worry as to whether or not it will be well fed. The stranger is then drawn into the tent, where he is immediately served whatever might be ready, while waiting for the feast. For a man on foot such attentions are no less.

The master of the tent keeps his guest company the entire day and leaves him only when it is time to retire. Never an indiscreet question —never these above all: "Where do you come from?" or, "Where are you going?"

There has never been an instance of an accident having befallen a man thus hospitably received, even were he a mortal enemy. However, upon the guest's departure, the master of the tent says: "Follow your good fortune." When the guest has gone, he who entertained him is no longer responsible for anything.

If, upon emerging from a hospitable feast, one passes by a *douar* and is seen, it is necessary to yield to the repeated offers which are made to one. Two tribes, however, are noted for their inhospitality: the Arbâa and the Oulad-Aïad.

On such alms and hospitality some men live their whole lives; they are the dervishes. Always at prayer, those pious personages are the objects of veneration on the part of everyone. "Take care not to do them an injury. God will punish you." Never is one of their demands denied.

At the side of these mendicant monks—who so vividly recall certain aspects of our Middle Ages—it is fitting, it seems to me, to place the *tolbas* (sages) and those experienced women who, today in the Sahara, fill the role which, at the period of which I speak, was played by magi-

cians, alchemists, sorcerers—all those personages of whom Tasso[4] and
Ariosto[5] have sung and of whom Cervantes[6] has made fun. It is to
those *tolbas* and to those old crones that men and women go to request
the philter—made of divers herbs and prepared with invocations and
grotesque and frightening practices—which is mixed into the food of
him or of her by whom one wishes to be loved. It is they who, on a
paper and on the bone of a dead man taken from the cemetery, write
with the name of your enemy some magic formulas and then bury the
bone and paper, which your enemy will join—"his belly filled with
worms." They will teach you the incantations which should be spoken,
upon closing a knife, to cut your enemy's life; those which should be
thrown into the stove where the food is cooking (of the household
to which you desire to bring trouble); those which should be written
on a copper plaque or on a flattened ball—which you will cast into the
stream from which the woman upon whom you desire to avenge yourself goes to drink. Seized by a dysentery as rapid as the stream's current,
she will die, or give herself to you; but to cure her it is necessary to
counteract the first spell with another.

Then comes an entire procession of specters, the ghosts of those who
died violent deaths, *tergou.* Hasten to say to the one that pursues you:
"Come, come! Go back in your hole, you are not frightening me. You
did not frighten me when you had your weapons!" He will follow you
for a little while, but then desist. If terror seizes you and you fly, you
will hear in the air the clatter of arms—behind, a horse pursuing you,
shouts, a terrifying uproar—until you fall, exhausted.

Go to Morocco, to the edges of the *Oued* Noun, twenty days' travel
east of Souss [and there] you will encounter the most celebrated sorcerers; a school of alchemists and necromancers, occult sciences, a
mountain which speaks; in a word, all the marvels of the world of
magic.

---

[4] Torquato Tasso (1544-1595): a great Italian epic poet, author of *Jerusalem
Delivered.*
[5] Ludovico Ariosto (1474-1533): epic and lyric poet, he too was one of Italy's
great poets.
[6] Miguel de Cervantes (1547–1616): born in Alcalá de Jenares, author of *Don
Quixote de la Mancha.*

It is at these superstitions that the lower class has arrived. The wealthy, the Marabouts, the *tolbas* of the *zaouïas*, the *cheurfaa* scrupulously follow religious precepts and read the Holy Books, but the masses are plunged in ignorance. Among them they know but two or three prayers and the gospel of the Prophet; praying is seldom done and ablutions are performed only when water is found.

The chieftains make an effort to remedy that ignorance. They have, even while traveling, the hour of prayer proclaimed by the muezzin. They establish schools under the tent, but a life of fatigue, of constant migrations and journeys soon causes the Arabs to forget the teachings of their childhood.

All take pleasure, however, in hearing such teachings recalled in a poetic guise by the *meddah*, bards, religious troubadours, who go about at feasts, singing the praises of the saints, of God, of the Holy War, accompanying themselves with tambourines and flutes. They are given numerous gifts.

15

ARISTOCRACY AMONG THE ARABS

The hand open (generous)
The saber drawn
And one sole word.

"Take a thornbush," the Emil Abd-el-Kader said to me one day, "and for one year water it with rosewater; it will not produce anything but thorns. Take a date palm, leave it without water, without cultivation; it will always produce dates."

According to the Arabs, that date palm represents the aristocracy and the thornbush the common people.

Among the Eastern peoples there is a belief in the power of blood, in the virtue of breeding. Aristocracy is regarded not only as a social necessity, but even as a law of nature. No one dreams, as among the peoples of the West, of revolting against that truth which, to the contrary, is accepted with placid resignation.

"The head is the head, the tail is the tail," the most humble of Arab shepherds will tell you. If the people among whom that axiom holds sway have chimeras by which they are tormented, there are, at least, ambitions from which they do not suffer. There are not to be seen, as among us, thousands of minds agitated by a perpetual delirium, seeking a means of transforming the tail into the head and the head into the tail.

Apart from that aristocracy of a remote and sacred origin which is composed of the descendants of the Prophet (the *chérifs*), there are among the Arabs two very distinct nobilities. One is the nobility of religion, the other the nobility of the sword. The Marabouts and the *djouad*, as those two breeds of men are called (deriving their eminence, the former from piety, the latter from courage; the former from prayer, the latter from combat), entertain an implacable hatred for each other. The *djouad* make to the Marabouts the reproaches which are freely addressed in all countries to religious orders aspiring to the management of human affairs. They accuse the Marabouts of ambition, intrigue, shady practices, and a perpetual cupidity for the good things of the world which is concealed under a feigned love of God and heaven. One of their proverbs says: "From the *zaouïa* a serpent always emerges."

The Marabouts, for their part, accuse the *djouad* of violence, of rapine, of impiety. That third accusation can place a terrible weapon in their hands. They are to their rivals that which the clergy of the Middle Ages was to that laic nobility whom an anathema could strike despite the formidable panoply of its warrior strength. If the *djouad* can make the people follow [them] by the memories of perils confronted, blood spilled, and military prestige, the Marabouts are armed with all the powerfulness of religious belief on the popular imagination. More than once a Marabout, loved or feared by the people, has imperiled the domination and even the life of a *djieud*.[1] It is that *djieud* whom I propose to depict today, because I desire to conduct to the desert those spirits who love to follow such excursions, and because the life of the desert is the warrior life par excellence. To show to the readers on the spot what an aristocrat of the Sahara is—in all the glory, all the sound, all the animation of his existence—it is necessary to portray what takes place under a grand tent at the moment when the day begins, from eight in the morning to noon.

Ancient poetry has often described that throng of petitioners who, in Rome, crowded the porticoes of patrician palaces. A grand tent in the desert is today as were, in their time and place, the sumptuous dwellings portrayed by Horace[2] and Juvenal.[3] Gravely seated on a

---

[1] *Djieud*: nobleman (singular of *djouad*).

[2] Horace [Quintus Horatius Flaccus] (65–8 B.C.): one of the greatest Roman lyric poets.

[3] Juvenal [Decimus Junius Juvenalis] (A.D. 60?–?140): Roman satirical poet.

carpet with that dignity in attitude which is the secret of the East, the
chieftain of the tribe receives, one after the other, all those who come
to invoke his authority. This one complains of a neighbor who has
tried to seduce his wife, that one accuses a man—richer than he—of
refusing to liquidate a debt. One wants to recover animals which were
carried off, another demands protection for his daughter whom a
brutal husband is crushing with ill-treatment. Sometimes a woman herself comes to complain that her husband does not clothe her, feeds her
badly, and denies her that which the Arabs, in the forceful originality
of their tongue, call the *share of God*. That last complaint is frequently
aired. Never, it is true, do women of the upper classes come to bring
out into the light of day the secret miseries of conjugal life. It is the
woman of the [common] people who demands the fulfillment of marriage. Persuaded that she is armed with a right, that she obeys a duty,
she presents herself with the intrepidity her conscience gives her of
being under the double protection of religion and the law.

The primary virtue of a chieftain is patience. He who listens to
these divers petitions lends an attentive ear to each. He studies ways
of curing wounds of any nature which are divulged to him.

"The man who is in power," according to an Arab phrase, "should
imitate the doctor who does not apply to all people the same remedies."

In these beds of justice, which recall the ancient courts in which our
early kings dealt with the private interests of their subjects, the Arab
chieftain employs all the wisdom which God has put into his mind and
the strength God has put into his will. To some he gives orders, to
others counsel. There is no one to whom he denies either his enlighten-
ment or in justice his support. The Arab chieftain has need not only
of the quality which Solomon asked of God; it is necessary that to
wisdom he add generosity and courage. The greatest eulogy which can
be spoken of him is that he has "his saber always drawn, his hand always open."

That charity, a little fastuous, but still of a noble and touching nature,
which Moslem law makes an obligation for all believers, is necessarily
practiced incessantly by the Arab chieftain. His tent should be the
refuge of the unfortunate; no one should die from hunger close to him,
for the Prophet has said: "God will accord His mercy but to the merci-

ful. Believer, give alms, even if it be nothing but the half of a date. Who gives alms today shall be replenished tomorrow."

If a warrior has lost the horse which constituted his strength, if a family has seen the flock which was its living carried off, it is to the chieftain, ever to the chieftain, that they address themselves. The desire for gain should never be one of the preoccupations of his mind. The Arab noble who, in so many ways, recalls the seigneur of the Middle Ages, differs essentially from our chevaliers by his aversion to gambling. Never do dice or cards while away the idle hours of the tent. An Arab chieftain may not gamble or make usurious loans. The only manner in which he sometimes makes his money work is by an indirect participation in a commercial enterprise. He gives a sum of money to a merchant, the merchant conducts business, and then, at the end of a few years, shares with his backer the profits which he has gleaned.

At the same time it should not be believed that wealth is held in disdain among the Saharians. There, as everywhere, it is, on the contrary, one of the indispensable requisites for power. Who falls into poverty also falls very quickly into obscurity and who attains fortune starts along the road to honors. But to follow the career of ambition, it is by arms rather than by industry that one should become wealthy. When a warrior has made a number of *razzias* which at the same time have won him silver and glory, he is called *ben deraou* (the son of his weapon) and he can aspire to the highest offices of his tribe. That leads us to the quality which should be the very foundation of a nobleman's soul— to bravery.

"Nothing," says Abd-el-Kader, "enhances the dazzling whiteness of a burnoose better than blood."

The Arab chieftain should be, as were our captains in times gone by, the bravest of his armed men. It is necessary that he be as outstanding in war games as in *fantasias*. His influence would be forever lost if his heart should be suspected of a weakness.

But it is reality, not the appearance of reality, that the Arabs appreciate. They admire a strongly tempered spirit—not the external appearance of a giant or an athlete: despite the generally widespread misconception that tall stature and physical strength produce on them a vivid impression, that is not so. They desire that a man be sturdy, impervious to thirst and hunger, able to withstand the greatest of fatigue; but they do not pay much attention to tall stature, to physical strength similar to that of our strong men at the fairs or of our porters. What they admire is agility, skill, and courage. Little does it matter to them if a man is tall or short; often, even upon regarding some colossus about whom one boasts to them, they can be heard to pronounce this sententious phrase: "What do height and physical strength matter to us? Let us see the heart! Perhaps there is nothing there but a lion's skin on a cow's frame!"

Despite that admiration of courage, a [certain] point of honor does not exist, however, among the Arabs as among us. To them there is no cowardice in withdrawing in the face of superior numbers, even in fleeing from an enemy weaker than oneself—when there is no interest in overcoming him. The Arabs often laugh among themselves at our chivalrous scruples. Even while loving the horses' breakneck gallops and the burning language of gunpowder, they want their combats to have, insofar as possible, a goal of practical utility. Full of ardor when luck leads them, they disperse and disappear as soon as it betrays them. Also, in their judgment of bravery, several essential differences exist between them and us. The admiration of courage does not impel them to an extreme [degree] of severity toward those in whom that virtue is lacking. Never will a coward gain high office in his tribe, but [neither] will he be an object of disdain. It will simply be said of him, with that absence of anger which fatalism often produces: "God has not willed that he be courageous; he is to be pitied and not blamed." It is demanded, however, that a fainthearted man compensate for his shortcomings by the wisdom of his counsel and, above all, by a constant generosity.

Boasting is treated with more scorn than [is] cowardice: "If you say that the lion is an ass, go and put a halter on him." Thus goes an Arab proverb which encounters frequent application.

Despite the ardor of their blood and the hyperbole of their language the Arabs desire for courage that dignity of silence which they esteem so highly. From that point of view they resemble not at all the nations with which they fought in the times of El Cid; no more do they resemble them from the point of view of individual combats. Among them today, individual combats are unknown. A tradition which goes back perhaps to the Crusades says, nonetheless, that in times gone by some illustrious chieftains have fought in single combat, but the oldest men among the tribes do not have any personal recollections of such encounters. When a man has offended one, revenge is taken, as in the sixteenth century, by assassination. Men can be found with an elastic conscience and a complaisant nature who, at very reasonable prices, will rid one of one's enemy. However, when someone is more avaricious of his gold than of his life, when he has his hand ready to strike and his purse slow to open, then he seeks an opportune moment and he himself falls upon the man from whom he received an insult. He kills or is killed. If he dies, often to someone else is bequeathed the debt of blood; for, not being under the safeguard of the duel, venegeance is no less alive and flourishing among the Arabs. The blood feud often passes from one generation to the next. In it are found those quarrels among races which have in bygone times reddened the pavements of Italian cities and bloody yet today the soil of a French island.

Generally, the causes of Arab vendettas are arguments over water, pastures, boundaries; the abduction of a young wife or a young girl; a jealous husband; a preferred rival; a woman who will not say yes. Whatever the rivalries among the chieftains, first the relatives, then the friends and partisans, and then the entire tribe and allied tribes finally espouse the quarrel. For the reason that dueling is unknown among the Arabs, it comes to pass that individual quarrels are settled by assassination and that, more and more incessantly nourished, hatreds continue forever. On the contrary, it is remarkable that the vendetta tends to efface itself from the customs of a people, as in Corsica and Italy, according to the measure in which dueling is accepted there. In that way, dueling has rendered an immense service to society, as it has substituted honest combat, face to face, for murder by stealth. For the rest, if it puts some families into mourning, it does not, at least, bequeath to them, like the vendetta, the dubious point of honor of eternal reprisals.

The vendetta is then individual or general, according to whether or not the offended interests are themselves individual or general. If, for whatever reason, there has been the death of a man in a tribe caused by the act of a chieftain or even of a subaltern of a neighboring tribe, the murderer can, upon paying the *dya* (the blood price) to the heirs of the victim, legally expunge the affair. The *dya* is the *Wehr-geld* of the Germans, with the difference that, apart from its legal nature, it has taken on among the Arabs, from its very beginning, a religious nature.

According to the *tolbas*, the *dya* goes back to the grandfather of Mohammed, Abd-el-Mettaleb, and was the indirect cause of the birth of the Prophet. Abd-el-Mettaleb, chieftain of the tribe of the Koreishites, had no son and in his despair he made this prayer to his God: "Lord, if You give me ten sons I vow to immolate one of them as a thank-offering."

God heard him and made him a father ten times. Abd-el-Mettaleb, faithful to his vow, resorted to lots to determine which son would be the victim and the lot fell on Abd-Allah. But, the tribe rising [in revolt] against that sacrifice, it was decided by the chieftains that instead of Abd-Allah, ten camels would be wagered, that lots would again be drawn until one fell on the child, and that, as many times as a lot was unfavorable, ten more camels would be added to the first. Abd-Allah was not ransomed until the eleventh test and one hundred camels were immolated in his stead. Sometime later God manifested that He had accepted that exchange favorably, for from Abd-Allah He caused Mohammed, His Prophet, to be born, and since that era the *dya*, the blood price of an Arab, has been fixed at one hundred camels. It can be understood, however, that that high price undergoes modifications according to circumstances.

There is scarcely an example of a murderer, who has paid the *dya*, being otherwise persecuted and the relatives of the dead man, even his children, have wholeheartedly accepted that indemnity. But if the murderer is too poor to pay it, or if the government has seen fit to take a hand in the affair, he is condemned to application of the Mosaic law: An eye for an eye, a tooth for a tooth, a life for a life.

When I was French consul in Mascara, close to the Emir Abd-el-Kader in 1837, I had the sad occasion, which is set forth here, to see the Mosaic law applied in all its severity:

[When] two children started fighting in the street their fathers intervened, went from insults to threats and [as] matters became more and more heated, one of the two drew his knife and stabbed his adversary, who fell dead. The dead man had five wounds, one on the right breast, another on the left breast, two in the belly and the fifth in the back. I stress these details for a specific purpose. A crowd had gathered and with it some *chaouchs* (police), who seized the murderer and conducted him to the *hakem* (magistrate) of the city. The *doulamas* (doctors of law) assembled at once and constituted themselves a tribunal. In less than half an hour, witnesses had been heard and the guilty man sentenced to undergo the [application of] the Mosaic law by the hand of his victim's brother. At a sign from the *cadi*, two *chaouchs* bound his wrists tightly with a cord made of *alfa* (fiber), one placed himself on the right, the other on the left and, preceded by the executioner, conducted him to the marketplace, thronged that day with two or three thousand Arabs. However horrible the strange drama to be enacted there would of necessity be, it was for me an occasion for making a singular study and I succeeded in overcoming the instinctive repugnance which I had had at first at the thought of being present at it.

When I arrived, the *chaouchs*, using clubs in the midst of the crowd, had driven it back to the limits of a large circle, around which it pressed, whose center was occupied by the executioner and the condemned man—the one with his knife in his hand, the other calm and as if indifferent to that which was going to take place there. Under the terms of the sentence, the murderer had to die from as many thrusts as he had given and receive them in the same order and in the same parts of the body in which his victim had received them.

When all was ready and the preparations were limited to the simple stage setting which I have described, a *chaouch* raised his club. It was the signal. The man with the knife instantly fell on the victim and struck him first on the right breast, then on the left, but undoubtedly without reaching the heart, for the wretched man shouted at him:

"Strike! Strike! But I do not believe that it is you who kills me! Only God kills!"

However, the torture continued with savagery while the sacrificed man—whose intestines escaped with waves of blood from two new wounds he had received in the belly—continued to insult his executioner.

There was one more thrust to give. The wounded man himself turned around and the blade of the knife disappeared entirely in his loins. He staggered but did not fall.

"That is enough! That is enough!" yelled the crowd. "He gave no more than five knife thrusts and he should not be given any more than that!"

The execution had, in effect, ended and the wretched man who had just borne it still had enough strength left to regain his house on foot. The [French] consulate doctor, M. Warnier, arrived there almost at the same instant and while he was mending by sutures the gaping edges of the two wounds the man had in his belly, the latter entreated him: "Oh! I pray you, heal me! It is said that you are a great doctor, prove it! Heal me so that I may kill that dog!"

But all was useless. The unfortunate man died in the night.

If the murderer is, on the contrary, the master of a grand tent, powerful enough so that his tribe uses circumspection in dealing with him and he refuses to pay the blood price, he will pay for that refusal sooner or later with his life. For, in the absence of justice, the vendetta will be sure to overtake him. But, from his death, war is born, as I have said. Examples of the vendetta which I could cite are numerous, and the following—because it is taken from the customs of a Saharian tribe, the Chamba, and from a people of the great desert, the Tuareg, two hundred leagues distant from one another—will give a fairer idea of these stubborn hatreds, of the thirst for vengeance which is always expressed by the very acts of violence themselves.

A party of Chamba, led by ben Mansour, chieftain of Ouargla, surprised, close to the Djebel-Baten, some Tuareg watering their camels in the Oued Mina, under the leadership of Khèddache, chieftain of the Djebel-Hoggar. An implacable hatred, whose original cause is unknown, so old is it, divides the Chamba and the Tuareg. The latter are, furthermore, in a perpetual state of vendetta with the Saharians, be it because they are Berbers and not Arabs, be it because they levy a crossing toll on the caravans from the Sudan.

Without preliminaries then, a savage fight ensued, and the Tuareg were routed, leaving ten of their dead, among which number was their chieftain, whom they found a few days later, decapitated. Ben Mansour had carried off the head and had displayed it, as a trophy of his victory, on one of the gates of Ouargla. Upon hearing that news there was mourning in [the tribe of the] Djebel-Hoggar and the following oath was sworn:

"May my tent be destroyed if Khèddache is not avenged!"

Khèddache left a widow of great beauty named Fetoum and a young son. According to custom Fetoum was to command, with the aid of the counsel of the great, while waiting until her son came of age to take office. Then one day, when the great were assembled in her tent: "My brothers," she told them, "the one from among you who brings me the head of ben Mansour will have me to wife."

That same evening all the young men of the mountainside, armed for war, came to tell her: "Tomorrow we shall depart with our servants to go in search of your wedding present."

At daybreak three hundred Tuareg, led by Ould Biska, cousin of Khèddache, found themselves en route toward the north; but scarcely had they taken up positions at the first halt when they saw coming on their heels some dozen mounted camels among which could be distinguished one more agile and more richly caparisoned than the others. It was instantly recognized as being that of Fetoum and it was indeed Fetoum who had come to ally herself with the small army. She was greeted with acclamations for—and perhaps she had done it on purpose —she seemed to have arrived there expressly to hold to her promise more promptly.

It was the month of May, all the ravines held water, all the sands had grasses; the season was favorable. At the halt on the eighth day, scouts came to announce that a strong faction of Chamba, led by ben Mansour, was conducting its herds toward the pastures of the Oued Nassa. However, those Chamba, themselves warned of the approach of the Tuareg, had turned sharply toward the north and gained the Oued Mzab. But that withdrawal movement was soon perceived and by a forced march of one day and one night, the Tuareg came to conceal themselves in ravines and thickets at only a few leagues from their enemies, unsuspecting on that occasion. The Tuareg remained there the entire day and, night having fallen, they regained the plain at the extended trot of their camels. Finally at midnight the barking of its dogs betrayed the *douar* they sought. An instant later, at the signal given by Ould Biska, the riders launched themselves [upon the camp] yelling the war cry. Of all the Chamba, only five or six escaped, and even one of these was overtaken by Ould Biska who, with one blow of his long lance, struck him in the loins. Carried away by his mare, the unfortunate horseman, losing his balance, swaying, hanging onto the saddle, went a few paces more. But he quickly succumbed and rolled on the sand, dragging down in his fall a boy of seven or eight whom he had hidden up until then under his burnoose.

"Ben Mansour! ben Mansour! Dost thou know ben Mansour?" Ould Biska demanded.

"He was my father and there he is!" the boy answered him, calm and standing upright by the body.

Fetoum arrived at the same moment, followed, surrounded, and pressed by a group of Tuareg.

"It was I who killed him!" Ould Biska shouted at her.

"And it shall be done according to my word," Fetoum assured him. "But, take your dagger, finish opening the body of the accursed, tear out the heart and throw it to the dogs."

While Ould Biska, kneeling and bent over the body, proceeded to carry out that order, Fetoum, lips compressed, quivering with a nervous tremble, avidly enjoyed that horrid spectacle. And when at last the salukis had finished their horrible repast, Fetoum, whose vengeance had been satisfied, without paying any attention to the booty which her servitors were piling up, or to the scattered flocks which they sought to gather together, remounted her *mahari* (racing camel) and gave the signal to withdraw.

With respect to the son of ben Mansour, he was spared, but he was abandoned on the spot. He remained there two days to weep with hunger, thirst, and the sun. On the third day he was found by some shepherds and taken to Ouargla where he still was in 1845.

Thus the dogs of the Tuareg ate the heart of the chieftain of the Chamba and it can be conceived that between them it will forever be the cause of a war without truce or mercy.

I shall not dwell further on these customs of such a savage nature. As a contrast, I prefer to depict some family scenes, beginning with the respect with which paternal authority is regarded among the Arabs. While the child is young, the tent belongs to him. His father is, in a way, the first among his slaves, his games are the delight of the family, his whims the life and gaiety of the home. But, just as soon as he reaches puberty, he is taught deference. He may no longer speak in front of his father or attend the same gatherings as he. That absolute respect which he must observe toward the head of his family he also owes his eldest brother. However, despite their aristocratic severity, Arab customs do not attain the somber rigor which patrician customs had in Rome. Thus a father would not condemn his son to death unless he had dishonored his bed; in any other case, the father would limit himself to banishing him from his presence.[4]

I have sketched rapidly and on a broad scale the character of Arab nobility. I shall now try to reproduce, in some of its most solemn moments, the life itself of a nobleman.

---

[4] "Arab children laugh at all danger. Instead of ceaselessly having behind him a mother, a nursemaid, whose principal task is to smooth out difficulties for him, the Arab child, as soon as he can walk, is left to himself. He is allowed to do what he dares.

"At what age does an Arab child learn to walk? It should be asked instead at what age does he not walk? The moment he is born he is laid naked on the ground and very quickly he tries to move. I have often seen children on the sand, aiding themselves with their arms and legs to go from one place to another. They are thus severely brought up until they are six or seven years old. They are then given a white cotton shirt which constitutes their entire garb. As soon as they gain a little strength their most important business is riding the horses, taking them to pasture and to water and launching them into breakneck gallops. The rest of the day they spend learning to sing or to dance, weapons in hand.

"The Arab urchin is then the happiest of all the urchins in the entire world. A singular thing is that, in their schools, they recite their lessons in chorus before a *thaleb* (tutor) from whom, however, mistakes and misdeeds seldom escape." (*Journey in Upper Asia*, by M. Pétiniaud, Inspector-General of Studs), commissioned by the French government to travel throughout Upper Asia, there to buy horses of pure Oriental blood. (*Horses of the Sahara*, E. Daumas)

On the day on which a boy is born in a grand tent there is great joy. Everyone comes to seek out the father of the newborn son to say to him: "May your son be happy!"

While the men press around the father, the mother also receives visits. The women of the tribe gather around her. Men and women have their hands full of gifts. The presents are in proportion to the fortune of each individual. From camels, sheep, and costly garments, to cereals and dates, all the treasures of the desert abound under the tent which God has just blessed. He who receives all these testimonies of affection and respect is obliged to provide a bountiful hospitality. Sometimes for twenty days he feeds and entertains all his visitors. The fêtes have in the desert the characteristic of grandeur inherent in all that which takes place in the solemn theater of primitive life.

As soon as the boy begins to develop he is taught to read and write, which is an innovation among the *djouad*. Formerly only the Marabouts practiced the art of letters. The man of the sword, like our baron of the Middle Ages, held all learning in contempt. It appeared to him that by cultivating his spirit an attack was being made on the stoutness of his heart. However, since they have seen among the least of our soldiers attainments which left bravery intact, the Arabs have changed their opinion, for those who have chosen to serve us have perceived that learning is a claim to our favors. Many from among them have finally said, with a melancholy resignation, these words which I gleaned one day: "Formerly we could live with ignorance, for calm and good fortune were in our midst; but, in these troubled times which we are obliged to undergo, it is necessary that science come to our aid."

Thus our [French] influence slowly accomplishes, [even] in the bosom of the desert, that civilizing work which among us is sometimes spoken of with a great deal of discouragement, sometimes with too much lightness.

The pursuit of letters does not cause to be neglected in Arab education the training of the horse or the maintenance of arms. As soon as a boy can stay on a horse, he is made to ride—first colts and then horses. When he begins to develop, he is taken hunting, made to do target practice, taught to bury his lance in the flanks of the wild boar. When he reaches sixteen or eighteen, when he knows the Koran and can practice fasting, he is wed. The Prophet has said: "Wed your youths. Marriage tames the gaze of the man and governs the conduct of the woman."

Up until then paternal tenderness has watched over the purity of the boy's ways with an incessant vigilance. He has never been left alone. A tutor or some servants have always accompanied his steps. Men of a dissolute life and women of abandoned conduct have been kept away from him. He should bring to her whom he has been given as a companion a sturdy body and a mind wherein filth has never entered. There is chosen for him a young girl of birth equal to his, with her reputation intact and, if possible, of great beauty. It is the women of his family who make sure of that point. They are permitted to make an examination in the tents where the marriageable girls live. At first [the couple] are betrothed and then the marriage takes place.

The first day of those [wedding] fêtes which, like those for a birth, are of long duration, is the day of "the carrying-off" (*nhar refoude*). Four or five hundred horsemen, magnificently clad, mounted on their most beautiful horses, armed with their most priceless weapons, and led by the parents of the groom, arrive at the tent of the betrothed. Some veiled women, mounted on camels and mules, accompany them. The youngest and prettiest girls in the tribe are chosen for that happy mission. The journey, which sometimes is a three-day march, is a continual *fantasia*. The horses gallop, the gunpowder thunders, and the women cast to the wind that long cry of love and joy which fills the souls of the sons of the desert with an indescribable sentimentality.

When that triumphal procession arrives, the father of the bride presents himself: "May you be well come, O guests of God!"

And then there are feasts and rejoicing until the following day when the journey is resumed. This time the bride is in the company, mounted on a mule or on a richly caparisoned she-camel. She has not said good-bye to her father. A somewhat genteel sentiment of modesty prevents her from appearing before him at the moment when her condition is going to change. It is also forbidden to her to see her elder brothers. Her life as a young girl is ended; from now on it is to another family that she will belong. At the moment of departure her mother embraces her tenderly and says: "You are leaving those from whom you came.

You are going away from the nest that has sheltered you for such a long time, from which you were launched to learn to walk, in order to reach the side of a man whom you do not know, to [enter] a society to which you are not accustomed. I counsel you to be a slave for him, if you desire that he be a servitor for you. Content yourself with little. Watch constantly over what his eyes might see and [be sure] that they never see bad actions. Watch over his food, watch over his slumber. Hunger leads to outbursts, insomnia brings bad humor. Be careful of his goods, treat his relatives and slaves with kindness. Be dumb concerning his secrets. When he is happy, do not show care. When he has cares do not be joyous. God will bless you."

While the nuptial journey takes place, the fiancé has prepared a richly adorned tent which he places under the guard of some friends. It is there that the bride enters with her mother and female relatives. She is offered a matchless banquet and all around her is celebrated a fête for which, from gunpowder to music, has been gathered all that which attracts joy in the desert. At ten o'clock in the evening, the groom slips into the tent, now deserted and silent. In the morning of the following day the mother of the bride receives from the groom's hands her daughter's shift. She unfurls that trophy before the eyes of all and says to the bride, both proud and embarrassed: "May God give you strength and health! You have not betrayed our hopes; you are a brave girl, you have never yellowed our faces."[5]

The fêtes of a wedding are often prolonged for three days and three nights. They recommence each time that the husband takes a new wife. Law permits an Arab chieftain to have four wives at the same time; but that number is not enough to satisfy the desires of those restless and voluptuous natures. It is in vain that, by a custom which recalls biblical ways, the Moslem husband may add concubines to his lawful wives; that tolerance is still insufficient. It is necessary that divorce come to the aid of insatiable and incessant appetite. An Arab chieftain is cited who has had twelve or fifteen lawful wives. Peace, as can be imagined, is far from prevailing in the households where the law sanctions such elements of disorder. Sometimes the tent is divided into two parts. One

[5] Red and light colors are, among the Arabs, a sign of good luck. Somber colors, particularly yellow, are an indication of misfortune. [Translator's note]

chamber is reserved exclusively for the women, the other belongs to the husband. The latter receives, in turn, each woman whom he chooses as the companion of his nights. However, that arrangement is rare; polygamous love, enclosed in one sole room, is ordinarily obliged to lose its luster, mystery, and modesty. Also it constantly comes to pass that terrible jealousies are secretly born, grow greater little by little, and end by exploding. Often a woman, a favorite out of all her companions, is stricken by a mysterious malady. She languishes, withers, and dies; a poison prepared by the hand of a rival has entered her veins. That is the sinister side of such customs. Crime there is coupled with voluptuousness.

One fact proves the immense role played by women in the Moslems' existence. Say to an Arab that he is a coward and he will tolerate the insult. If he is a coward it is because God has willed it thus. Accuse him of being a thief, he will smile; in his eyes theft is sometimes a meritorious action. Call him *tahan*, a word which the language of Molière can translate only with a terse forcefulness, and you will kindle in his soul an anger which cannot be extinguished except by blood. The only man whom an Arab should never forgive is he who has acquired the right to hurl in his face someday that malevolent epithet.

As soon as he is married the nobleman of the desert enters upon a new life, into a sphere of personal action. He is emancipated; not absolutely, always, if he is not the head of the tent, if he is not the master of his property, if his father is still living. However, even under those conditions, he will be numbered henceforward in his tribe as a man-at-arms and counsel and he will finish through experience the training of a great lord, up until that time outlined by the custom of good examples and good advice. He already has his followers, his horses, his salukis, his falcons, all his equipment for war and the chase.

His followers are the young men of his own age, the courtiers of his future. His horses have been chosen from among those which bear good luck (*mesaoudin*) and [are] of the truest genealogy. His salukis —he himself has fed them on dates crushed in milk, with *couscous* from his meal. He has trained them and, while the common curs of the tribe bark during the night at the hyenas and jackals, the salukis lie at his feet under the tent and even on his bed. His falcons have been bred in front of his eyes by his falconer (*biaz*) and he himself has taken care to accustom them to his cry of flight and recall.

Amid his equipment for war and the chase there stand out rifles from Tunis or Algiers, damascened, silver-mounted, the wood encrusted with mother-of-pearl or coral; the sabers with chased-silver scabbards; saddles embroidered in gold and silk on velours or morocco leather. To complete the equipment we shall enumerate, furthermore, the saddlebag (*djebira*) adorned with leopard skin; the spurs (*chabir*), silver-plated, encrusted with coral; the *medol*, a high, broad straw hat with a panache of ostrich plumes; the cartridge clip (*mahazema*) in morocco leather piped with silk, gold, and silver.

One day, when his father shall have paid "the tax which God levies on all heads," that vast tent (*khreima*) will be his with all its luxurious furnishings, rugs, pillows, sacks of jewels, silver cups; provisions for the chase, for war; for all the family to the number of twenty-five or thirty, master and servants. To him will belong, furthermore, that stallion and those mares hobbled within sight of the tent. Those eight or ten Negroes and Negresses, those stores of wheat, barley, dates, honey, prudently sheltered from a coup in a *ksar* (village), those eight or ten thousand sheep, those five or six hundred camels scattered at a distance in pastures under the care of shepherds wandering along with them. His fortune could then be reckoned at 25,000 or 26,000 *douros* (125,000 or 130,000 francs).

At the age at which we left him, nineteen or twenty years old, he does not yet have to preoccupy himself with the administration of that fortune. Today, he is a man of pleasure. In times of peace, on horseback, followed by his friends, and some servants riding camels, who have his salukis on leashes or may even be carrying them in front of them, when he arrives at distant pastures to visit the herds, it is an occasion for a chase of the ostrich, the gazelle, the *bekeur-el-ouhach* (antelope), according to the terrain and the season. Should his scouts, making reconnoiters, have signaled ostriches, the hunters, gaining ground, will enclose them in a circle, at first immense, but which they tighten little by little until, having them in sight, they fall on them at top speed, yelling hunting cries. Each one chooses his victim, follows it in all the doublings of its erratic course, and overtakes it when, fluttering its wings to aid its legs, it is hard-pressed and he finishes it with a blow on the head from a club—for a bullet would bloody and soil the plumage.

If it is a matter of gazelles, which often, so numerous are they, from a distance resemble the herd [of camels] of a tribe, the horsemen advance toward them, while the servants who follow muzzle the dogs to prevent their giving tongue. At a distance of a quarter of a league the dogs are loosed upon them, the servants crying, exciting the dogs: "My brother! My friend! There they are! Do you see them?"

The hunters follow at a canter, but the gazelles have fled and it is not until after a headlong course of two or three leagues that the salukis enter the herd of which the horsemen—this time launched into a breakneck gallop and disposed in a semicircle—cause the mass to fall back toward the dogs. Each saluki has made a choice of one of the most beautiful stags. The latter leaps, bounds, turns on its enemy, fights with its horns, clears him with a single leap but, soon, it bellows plaintively and feels its legs stiffen. It is its death-cry. With one bite on the nape of the neck the remorseless saluki breaks the vertebra and the hunter comes up. He bleeds the stag *in the Name of God*! (*bessem Allah*!).

But the aristocratic and seigneurial chase par excellence is hawking. The falcon bred under the tent on a perch to which it is tied by an elegant morocco leather cord is carefully fed by the chieftain himself and trained by him. Its hood and harness are emblazoned with silk, *filaly* and small ostrich plumes. Its jesses are embroidered and ornamented with tiny silver tinkling bells. As soon as its training has been completed by chases after a lure, its master invites his friends to the first flight. All are faithful to the rendezvous, well mounted. The chieftain leads, one bird on his shoulder and another on his wrist protected by a long, skin gauntlet.

"Next to a *goum* departing for war, nothing is as lovely," said the Emir Abd-el-Kader, "as a departure to go hawking."

The horses neigh and depart in great bounds, the horsemen scatter among the thickets, beating the mottes of *alfa*; a hare springs up, the falcon is instantly unhooded and his master cries to him: "*Ha ou*! [There it is!]"

The intelligent bird soars almost out of eye range. It could be be-

lieved that it planned betrayal (to escape) but suddenly it plummets on
its prey with the speed of lightning, grips the hare in its talons and
stuns or even kills it. When its master arrives at a gallop he finds it
eating the eyes. If it is a *houbara* (bustard) which the hunters have
flushed, the falcon follows it in its flight— the bustard soars, the falcon
soars with it, both are momentarily lost in space beyond the sight of the
waiting hunters. Then suddenly they are seen to plummet, spinning,
the bustard's wings are broken. Its vanquisher keeps above it so that,
say the Arabs, only the bustard will suffer the impact of that terrifying
fall and the falcon will spare itself from it.

These violent sports mold the aristocracy for the work of war and
razzias. Has a caravan been pillaged, have the women of the tribe been
insulted, have water and pasture been disputed? The chieftains gather,
war is decided upon. All the chieftains of allied tribes are written to
and all arrive on the indicated day with their *goums* and infantrymen.
It is solemnly sworn, in the name of a venerated Marabout, to lend
mutual assistance and not to be but one and the same rifle. The following day, without further delay, everything stirs and is set in motion—
that includes the women, borne on camels, in palanquins which are not
always discreetly enough closed. It is a picturesque horde of horses and
warriors, the infantrymen forming a band apart. On the flanks of the
column the young men, the most hot-headed, scatter out as scouts, or,
more often, as hunters, for should a gazelle, an antelope, an ostrich, or
even a hare go bounding off, they will launch themselves behind their
salukis and more than one daring [man] will know how, profiting
from the disorder, to slip close to a palanquin where he is expected and
into which he climbs with the help of a well-paid servant, not to get
down again until nightfall at the first halt.

For its part, the enemy tribe makes its preparations. After four or
five days of travel the parties are in each other's presence. The scouts
are the first to meet and begin the hostilities with insults like those of
the heroes of Homer. Little by little battle is joined by small bands of
fifteen or twenty men, and shortly everything becomes livelier and goes
into action. The melee becomes general, all the rifles fire together, all
throats are provoked by yells and imprecations, and finally there is
hand-to-hand combat with sabers.

The hour comes, however, when that one of the two tribes which has lost more men, above all, more leaders and horses, is obliged to give way and fall back on its camp. It is a disorderly devil-take-the-hindmost rout in which the bravest still face the enemy from time to time to send a few random bullets at him. It is not unheard of that then the chieftain, in despair, saber in hand, launches himself into the melee and falls, gloriously cut down.

After the victory, the pillaging. One loots an infantryman, another an overthrown horseman; this one disputes a horse with that one, with another a Negro, a beautiful rifle, a costly *yatagan*[6] and, thanks to that disorder, more than one loser can save his women, his horses, and his most prized objects.

Upon return to its territory the tribe is received with a fête wherein joy is transmuted into festivities and offerings to the Marabouts whose influence it is important to take into consideration. The greatest hospitality is given to the allies, to whom there is also paid the price of their services (*zebeur*). They are then escorted for three or four hours of travel in the direction of their lands and leave is finally taken upon renewing the oath to "come to the aid of each other in the morning, if it is demanded in the morning and at night, if it is demanded at night."

In the measure that he grows older, the Arab acquires more gravity; each gray hair in his beard leads him to more serious ideas; he frequents more willingly the men of God and becomes more generous toward them; he becomes more devout. He is seen less often in the chase, at weddings, *fantasias*. His occupations as chieftain, furthermore, leave him less free time. He must administer justice, increase his wealth, raise his children, deal with alliances. Nevertheless, the chivalresque spirit of his youth only slumbers in him. When the gunpowder speaks because of an offense to his tribe, he will not remain in the tent.

"A very fortunate event," he would say, "to die like a man in combat, and not like an old woman."

Certain great families pride themselves highly on there being no memory of even one of their ancestors having died in his bed. If, however, he eludes that desired end, as soon as he feels Death's hand on

---

[6] *Yatagan:* a long knife or short saber common among the Mohammedans.

him, he has all his friends come, for among the people of the desert friends are bidden to all the great acts of human existence.

"My brothers," he will say to them, when it is possible for him to speak, "I shall never see you again in this world. I am just passing through this earth and I die in the fear of God."

Then he recites the *chehada*, that is to say the symbolic last act of Moslem faith: "There is only one God and Mohammed is God's envoy."

If his lips refuse to speak these sacred words, one of those present takes his right hand and raises the index finger. That sign, to which the dying man clings with all the strength which still remains in his mortal coil, is a witness rendered to the unity of God. When he has achieved the *chehada*, he may die in peace.

Human rituals are not lacking for the Arab chieftain, above all, not for the warrior slain when fighting for his tribe. He is wrapped in a white shroud and he lies in state on a carpet with raised edges. The *neddabat*, that is to say the women who among the Saharians replace the mourners of antiquity, sit around the body, their cheeks blackened with soot and their shoulders draped with tenting material or sacks of camel's-hair. A few paces from them a slave holds by the bridle the war or *fantasia* mare, the dead man's favorite. From the *kerbouss* (pommel) of the saddle hang a long rifle, a *yatagan*, pistols, and spurs. A little farther away the horsemen, young and old mute with grief, are seated in a circle on the sand, their *haïks* raised to just beneath their eyes, their hoods and burnooses lowered on the forehead.

The *neddabat* sing to a lugubrious rhythm the following lamentations:

> Where is he?
> His horse has come, he has not come;
> His saber has come, he has not come;
> His spurs are there, he is not there.
> Where is he?
> It is said that he is dead in his day,
>   stricken right to the heart.
>
> He was a sea of *couscous*.
> He was a sea of gunpowder.

> The seigneur of men,
> The seigneur of horsemen,
> The defender of camels,
> The protector of strangers;
> It is said that he is dead in his day.

The wife of the dead man:

> My tent is empty,
> I am chilled.
> Where is my lion?
> Where to find his equal?
> He never struck but with the saber.
> He was a man for black days;
> Fear is in the *goum*.

The *neddabat*:

> He is not dead! He is not dead!
> He has left you his brothers,
> He has left you his children.
> They will be bulwarks for your shoulders.
> He is not dead; his soul is with God.
> We shall see him again one day.

After these funereal lamentations, the *adjaïze* (old crones) take charge of the body, bathe it carefully, place camphor and cotton in all the natural orifices and wind it in a white shroud sprinkled with water from the well of Zem-zem,[7] scented with benzoin. Four relatives of the dead man then lift by its four corners the rug on which he is laid and take the road to the graveyard, preceded by the imam, the Marabouts, the *tolbas*, and followed by the cortege. The leaders chant in a grave tone: "There is but one God!"

The mourners answer in chorus: "And our Lord Mohammed is God's envoy!"

Resignation momentarily calms despair and not one cry, not one sob trouble these common prayers, these professions of the dead man's faith, repeated for him by the pious assembly. Arrived at the cemetery,

---

[7] Zem-zem: a well whose water comes from Paradise and which the pilgrims bring back from Mecca.

the pallbearers lay their sacred burden on the edge of the grave and the imam, after having placed himself by the side of the body, surrounded by the Marabouts, chants in a loud and sonorous voice the *salat el djenaza* (burial prayer):

> Homage to God Who causes death and Who causes life!
> Homage to Him Who raises the dead!
> It is to Him that all honor, all grandeur reverts; it is to Him alone that command and power belong. He is above all! That this prayer be also for the Prophet Mohammed, for his relatives, for his friends! O my God! Watch over them and accord them Thy mercy as Thou hast accorded it to Ibrahim [Abraham] and to his, for it is to Thee that glory and homages belong!
> O my God! N— was Thy worshipper, the son of Thy slave, it is Thou Who hadst created him, Thou Who hadst granted him the blessings which he has enjoyed. It is Thou Who caused him to die, it is Thou Who shouldst raise him.
> Thou art best informed of his secrets and his prior dispositions. We come here to intercede for him, O my God! Deliver him from the bitterness of the tomb and fires of hell. Forgive him, accord him Thy mercy. Cause that the place which he is to occupy be honorable and spacious. Bathe him with water, with snow, with hail, and cleanse him from his sins, as a white garment is cleansed from the impurities which can have sullied it. Give him a better dwelling than his own, better relatives than his own, and a more perfect wife than his own. If he was good, make him better; if he was wicked, forgive him his wickedness, O my God! He has taken refuge with Thee and Thou art the best of all refuges. It is a poor man who has come to seek Thy munificence and Thou art too wealthy to deny him and make him suffer.
> O my God! Strengthen the voice of the dead man at the moment when he is giving Thee an account of his actions and do not inflict a punishment beyond his strength to bear. We ask this through the intercession of Thy Prophet, of all Thine angels and of all Thy saints.
> *Amin!*

"*Amin!*" say all those present, genuflecting.

Then the imam resumes:

> O my God! Forgive our dead, our living ones, those of us who are present, those of us who are absent, our little ones, our great ones.

Forgive our fathers, all those who preceded us, and all Moslems! Those whom Thou wilt bring to life again, bring to life in the faith. And those among us whom Thou wilt cause to die, let them die true believers! Prepare us for a good death and may that death give us rest and the favor of beholding Thee! *Amin*!

The prayer being ended and while the *tolbas* recite the *salat el mokteâat*, the body is lowered into the grave, the face turned toward Mecca. Large stones are fitted around it and everyone present makes it a point of honor to throw in a little earth. The gravediggers level the surface of the grave and cover it with thorny shrubs to protect it from hyenas and jackals.

It is now time to return and all retrace their steps to the *douar*, with the exception of a few women, the friends or relatives of the deceased, who, bowed down with sorrow over the grave, speak to the dead man and question him and bid him farewell, as if they thought he could hear them. At last the *tolbas* and Marabouts exclaim: "Come now, women! Withdraw. Trust in God and leave the dead in peace to settle with Azrael.[8] Cease your tears and lamentations. Death is a tax levied upon our heads. All of us must pay it. There is no alternative, but neither is there any injustice in this event. God alone is eternal. What! Should we accept the will of God when it brings us joy and refuse it when it brings us sorrow? Depart! Your cries are an impiety."

They understand those words and with their hands before their eyes they go forth from the cemetery, but at every step they turn around to renew their last farewells to him whom they will never see again until the Day of Final Judgment.

The foregoing funeral oration is pronounced in the desert over every grave. The monotony of habit is the servant of grandeur. If the Arab manners are deficient in variety they are, at least, solemn and imposing.

---

8 "The Angel of Death": as soon as a man yields his last breath, Azrael is sent by God to strike the balance between the deceased's good and bad actions.

CONCERNING RESIGNATION: ISLAM

My virtue is resignation;
My fortune a disdain for wealth;
My happiness the hope of another life;
And should misery come to clutch my throat,
Not for that would I glorify God the less.

To study the customs of a people with care it is often necessary to go back to the etymology of certain words which, in themselves, suffice to rectify erroneous ideas and to make clear the truth being sought. I have always done well with that method and I resort to it afresh today to deal with an important question of Moslem religion.

At first I asked myself what the word *islam* meant, from which comes the name of Islam. I see that the Arabic verb *eslem*, derived from the verb *selem* (to deliver, to save) has, as an abstract noun, or as an infinitive, the word *islām*, which signifies submission to the will of God and, as a consequence, resignation.

Islam is, then, the Religion of Resignation. From Moslem (*muslim*), we have made Mussulman, giving it a form borrowed from the Turkish language, indicating a man resigned to God. It is evident then, from the preceding, that the fundamental principle of Islam is resignation. From resignation to fatalism there is but one step, I admit; but from resignation to trust in God the distance is no greater. The difficulty for the Moslem is then that of not exceeding the limit which has been set for him, of maintaining himself between fatalism which kills and hope which vivifies.

Such a rule of conduct is undoubtedly difficult to follow. Thus there should not be any astonishment because the lower classes of Moslem society have leaned more toward fatalism, impelled perhaps by the policy of their princes who, at certain times, have had need of kindling religious passion. But, if one sticks to facts, to teachings, and tradition, it is easy to realize that, for the educated and intelligent classes, if Islam demands resignation to an accomplished fact, it does not impose blind fatalism, which is a submission to a fact [still] to come. These principles appear to me to be in accord with the legends on which I am going to base the idea I have formed of the Moslem religion. These legends, the precepts, the maxims, the thoughts familiar to the Arab people, which we count on intermingling, stem from two great sentiments and, according to us, could be termed the decompound analysis of Moslem fatality: resignation and trust.

Resignation is the faith in that which it holds of austerity and discipline. Trust is faith again, but in that which it holds of enthusiasm and expectation. I will try to shed light on the two sides of the same coin. My help with that task will be the answer to the appeal which I have always addressed—each time that I desired to shed light on a new part of Moslem civilization—to the traditions, to the memories, and even to the language of the people who were the object of my studies. The method which I have employed up to the present, and which the public has encouraged, is that of allowing the Arab nature to portray itself, so to speak, in my writings. I resort to that method more than ever today. I hold the pen; I shall leave the words to those whose spirit I desire to make known.

Ask the Prophet to define resignation for you and here is what he will reply: "Resignation consists of being at all times contented with the lot which God has fashioned for us; of never coveting honors or the goods of others. It is a treasure so rich," he adds, "that it cannot rust."

God has said: "I would never deny paradise to a human creature, of whatever sex, provided that he be of the Moslem religion. But resignation is imperatively demanded by that life."

Ben-el-Haret, as a young man, had started off in search of fortune. He was obliged at the end of a long journey to rest amid some ruins. While gazing about him he saw a few lines of writing, traced on a large wall. He read them and here is what was written: "I see you seated in front of me and I understand the cares of which you are the prey. Hope in God. It is He Who holds the key to all treasures. Cast away your sorrows in His riches and you will find yourself well."

The young man, enlightened by the unexpected revelation, started off anew, saying: "O my God! It is to Thee that it falls to guide me; I was nothing but a fool."

Resignation is confounded with trust in that simple story, stamped with the consolatory ideal sought by men of all countries and of all creeds.

The following sketch breathes a love and an understanding of poverty which recalls the habits, the instincts, and the inspirations of the Christian soul.

One day Hamadi-ben-Ilanifa offered four thousand *douros* to his friend Saoud-ben-el-Taï, whom he found in dire straits. That sum came from an inheritance. "Accept this money," he said to his friend. "It comes from a man who was rich and generous."

Saoud answered him: "If I were disposed to receive such gifts, I would hasten to receive yours, as much out of respect for the dead as of deference to the living. But do not wish me ill if I refuse. I have sworn to continue to live as in the past, contenting myself with little."

We have just seen how the Moslem religion recalls ours by an austere manner of comprehending an entire facet of life. We shall see it draw closer yet by a kind of ascetic impetuosity, in great and sudden inspirations.

Abd-Allah-ben-el-Merzouk became intoxicated one day to the point that he could not say his prayer, and fell asleep. A very pious slave whom he owned applied a burning ember to the soles of his feet. He awakened with a start, terror-stricken.

"How," the slave then said to him, "will you be able to endure the pain of eternal fire if you cannot even bear the fire of this perishable world?"

Abd-Allah arose, said his prayer, freed his slave, and gave away as alms everything he owned, confiding to God, furthermore, the care of providing for his wants.

God said to Sid-na-Moussa (our lord Moses) : "Do you know why I give riches to the poor in spirit?"

"No," replied Sid-na-Moussa.

"Well, it is to make it understood by all that I do not love sensible spirits."

There is in those words something which at first astounds our reason, makes it revolt, and impels us to ask ourselves if we have not been misled by some flaw in translation. But a few minutes of reflection will lead us to understand the profound meaning hidden in the words received by the Prophet. Here the Bible and the Koran meet; our religion and the Moslem religion encounter in their common origin a striking harmony. *"Human wisdom is naught but folly,"* according to the Book of Ecclesiastes. It is evidently of that false wisdom that Arab tradition desires to speak upon expressing the aversion of the Creator to "sensible spirits." There exists in the human soul a wisdom superior to all the counsels of prudence, soaring above all illusions, all appearances, of which reason so often leads us to be the dupes. That natural and superior science is the relinquishment of believing souls to the mysterious decrees which govern it.

See the bird of ephemeral traces. It does not sow, it does not reap, it does not carry any provisions with it and yet God purveys its subsistence. Our stomachs, you will tell me, are larger than those of birds. So be it; but I shall answer you that they are very inferior in capacity to those of ruminants which, however, God also takes care of feeding.

Here again are words wherein it could be said that Christian breath is exhaled, here can be found the sacred text translated into immortal verse by the author of *Athalie*.[1] Were we to wish to arrive at that which

---

[1] Jean Racine (1639–1699): French dramatist. He occupies a unique position as the exemplar of French classicism par excellence. Athaliah, Queen of Judah, had the males of the royal family murdered. However, she was thwarted by her step-daughter Jehosheba, who hid away a baby son of Ahaziah. Some years after, Jehosheba and her husband effected a coup d'etat in favor of this baby, Jehoash II. Athaliah they killed. These events are the subject of Racine's *Athalie*. [Translator's note]

the development of these thoughts can give of the utmost delicacy and greatest subtlety we would continue:

An imam, after having prayed, one day asked of an Arab of the desert how he managed to live.
"Begin your prayer anew," the latter told him.
"Why?"
"Because he who is uneasy about his sustenance has doubted the Creator."

Questioned on the same subject another Arab answered: "*If I did not eat until after I had tormented myself to learn from where I was going to get my food, I would never eat.*"

> I would that, at that age,
> One would go out of life as from a banquet,
> Thanking one's host and making one's departure.

Thus he expresses himself, he who, perhaps, from among our poets, has best been able to enliven his works with the purest and most gracious spirit of wisdom.[2] That touching resignation which La Fontaine recommends to us in a simple and suave tongue, Arab tradition teaches us upon making use of the same imagery. Let us listen:

I agree that man, in this life, is considered as one who is invited to a feast. He can taste a dish passing by in front of him; he should not dream of the one which is going away.

Brahim-ben-Chekik said one day, in a gathering of friends: "*If I have something to eat, I eat, and if I do not have anything, I wait in patience.*"
"That is not enough," one of his listeners said to him. "*It is necessary to do what I do; if I have with which to do it, I eat and share; if I have nothing, I yet give thanks to God.*"[3]

---

[2] Jean de La Fontaine (1621–1695): French poet, author of fables. His masterpiece was *Fables Choisies: Mises en Vers.* The fables place La Fontaine . . . as a master of perfection in verse, fidelity to human nature, and narrative skill. [Translator's note]
[3] The Arabs never ask of what religion you are; they even avoid all conversation on the subject and yet—I cannot reiterate it often enough—all their actions and all their words are stamped with the thought of God. How many times, during my travels, has it not happened to me to see, at the rising of the sun, Arabs kneeling on their cloaks, with their weapons beside them, their heads turned toward Mecca, praying—in the midst of the desert and the unpeopled countryside, between the sky and the sand—with a fervor as touching as it is free of all affectation. I own

Here, resignation joins itself to that supreme word, to that crowning of all virtues, to charity.

El Moussalli, returning home at the end of the day, found nothing to eat. His family did not even have a lamp to combat the shadows which were beginning to invade his dwelling. He began to weep for joy, exclaiming: *"What then is that good fortune worth to me?"*

It can be seen that through resignation the Arab can even arrive at that which mystic joys contain of the most superhuman; to the grateful acceptance, triumphant even, it can be said, over the ills which the hand of God allows to fall on him.

God has given men different natures to prevent the discord among them that is born from the aspirations of all toward the same goal. If that variety did not exist in their hearts they would all be devoured by the same passion for the supreme rank, riches, pleasures, and goods of this life. Public peace and private tranquility would be equally impossible.

Behold the nomadic Arab! He is camped on a vast plain where he hears nothing but the yelp of the jackal and the voice of the Angel of Death.

His dwelling consists of nothing but some lengths of cloth which the absence of wood forces him to spread with bones from carrion.

The sun is his hearth, the moon is his lamp.

The flesh and wool of the sheep, behold that which provides his daily meal; behold that which serves for his clothing.

Should he desire to make some extraordinary feast it is necessary that he hunt the ostrich and the gazelle.

Be he ill, he has no other beverages but milk and water; no medications other than simples.

His dwelling can never crumble; he lies down where night overtakes him.

He has before his tent his camels, his horse, and his dog; under his tent his children and his wives, whose most luxurious garb consists of some pieces of silver threaded together.

---

that the profound conviction of those people has very often elicited my astonishment, perhaps my admiration. *Everything comes from God.* That is their constant idea and that idea inspires in them, under any circumstances, a sublime resignation (M. Pétiniaud, Inspector-General of Studs, *Journey in Upper Asia*).

The scent of tar, of the gazelle, and of the plants of the desert are his only perfumes.

That man, however, is the true Moslem; he has turned aside his heart and his eyes from this world; he is contented with his lot and he glorifies God.

Avidity is indigence.

Fortune is a disdain for wealth.

What philosophy contains of the most vivifying assuredly bursts forth in these words wherein there can also be felt to glide a ray of faith: *"If you wish to rejoin me,"* the Prophet said to his wife, Aycha, *"furnish yourself always with the provisions of a simple traveler and never frequent the rich. With regard to my people, the beginning of their fortune will be obedience and the abandonment of all earthly ties. The signs of their decadence will be avarice and cupidity."*

Such are the precepts on which the Moslem religion rests. Could it be concluded, by chance, from what has just been read that an apologetic thought for the good side of that religion might have crossed my mind? I cannot suppose it for an instant. I have always believed that it behooves a victorious nation to learn, in order to govern better, the creed and the ways of the people it has conquered. For a long time I have dedicated patient efforts to have light shed on the most intimate parts of Arab society. It is, quite simply, one of those efforts which should be perceived in the preceding work.

But these principles, it will be said to us, perhaps, which you represent as being so alive, armed with an authority so powerful, among the Moslems [are], however, practiced by very few of them today. It is with the Arab people as with other peoples: when a forceful and wise government presides over its destinies, among such a people the precepts inscribed in its laws can be seen to be honored. When it becomes the prey of anarchy, it treats the most sacred texts as dead letters. That is not the history of one country only and one era only—it is the history of all countries and of all times.

17

THE CHAMBI IN PARIS

[In] the land, where your pride
suffers, quit it although its walls
be built of rubies.

Whereas among us poetry is the gift of a few, the privilege of a few
spirits, a rare and exquisite flower which belongs only to a certain soil,
among the Arabs it is everywhere. It enlivens, in the land of space,
sun, and danger, both the spectacles of nature and the scenes of human
life. It is a treasure upon which all come to draw, from the shepherd
whose flocks dispute on a burning soil some tuft of withered grass to
the master of the grand tent who gallops in the midst of clattering
goums on a richly caparisoned horse. It is a fact of which all those
are aware who have, as I have, led for a long time the Arab life.
The persons who are still in their apprenticeship to African ways often
believe that that which they have heard repeated so many times concerning Arab poetry is an exaggeration. They fear to put to the test an
already preconceived opinion, to allow themselves to be imposed on by
that which is termed, I believe, conventional, in the language of artists.
I had noted such tendencies in an officer of the spahis whom I would
like to introduce [now] in the interests of truth.[1] M. de Molènes,

---

[1] The spahis were a corps of Algerian native cavalry in the French army, normally
serving in Africa, half of whose officers below the rank of captain and all of that
rank or above were French. The corps was originally composed largely of Turkish
spahis serving in Algeria at the French conquest in 1830. [Translator's note]

whose name, today wholly military, will nevertheless revive perhaps some literary recollections among my readers, was arguing one morning in my office [about] the poetic gifts of the Arab people when our discussion was interrupted by a visit of an unusual and unexpected nature.

The man who presented himself to our eyes wore the burnoose and the *haïk*; he was a Chambi.[2] He belonged to that breed of audacious traffickers who brave the serpent's bite, the tempests of sand, and the lances of the Tuareg, "those veiled brigands" of the desert,[3] to go as far as the Sudan to seek elephant tusks, gold dust, and perfumed essences. I had already encountered during the course of my life in Africa that constant and placid traveler who answers you with the serene melancholy of fatalism when you question him about his wandering destiny: "I go where God leads me."

On this occasion the Chambi had come to take to the Jardin des Plantes, on the orders of General Pélissier,[4] two of those celebrated *maharis* (racing camels) which the warriors ride in the Sahara and which attain, it is said, a speed to shame the most generous of coursers.

Had the Prophet wished to provide an irrefutable witness to my words on the ineradicable poetry of his people, he could not have sent me a more opportune guest than the Chambi. He, who would serve as living proof of my arguments, was not, in truth, one of those *tolbas* who glean in the learned retreat of the *zaouïa* inspirations unknown to the common herd, from the mysterious sources of sacred books. Nor was he one of those warriors followed by horsemen, preceded by standards, surrounded by musicians, who can extract from an existence of éclat and noise an entire exceptional gamut of emotions. No, he was

---

2 A member of the large Chamba tribe in the Sahara.

3 The Tuareg, "those veiled brigands," are a Moslem Berber people, nomads of the Sahara. Among the most highly civilized peoples of Africa, they have preserved their ancient alphabet. Their social organization is one of hereditary classes. The upper classes, organized in tribes, convoy caravans, and, until subdued by France, were feared as raiders. Menial labor is performed by non-Tuareg servants, formerly by captive slaves. Tuareg men go veiled, while the women are unveiled and enjoy respect and freedom. The fiercely independent Tuareg resented European hegemony in Africa and long resisted conquest according to Brian Gardner, in *The Quest for Timbuctoo,* London, 1968.

4 Aimable Jean-Jacques Pélissier (1794–1864): veteran of French campaigns in Algeria. He was made Duke of Malakoff, and, in 1860, named Governor General of Algeria. [Translator's note]

a man of the lowest class, who, here [in France], would be a peddler in our countryside.

"Well, now," I said to my interlocutor, "I will wager that if I question this obscure inhabitant of the desert at random I shall instantly withdraw from his brain songs which, perhaps, the best of our poets might envy."

The challenge was accepted. The questioning began. Let it be judged what came of it.

First there came a religious song. It is necessary to repeat among the Arabs what the ancient poets said: "Let us begin with the gods." There, that beginning and that ending of our life—that is to say, divine religion—is never forgotten. That God, with Whom it would appear that life in the open air makes contact more frequent, His presence more felt, and His power much closer, is always invoked by nomadic singers. The Chambi did not delay long consulting his memory. After having hummed, to get in tune, one of those airs as monotonous as the desert's horizon, with which the Arabs while away their time traveling on camelback, here is what he recited to us:

> Invoke him whom God has overwhelmed with his mercies
> O all you who listen to us!
> Believe in his ten companions
> The first to compose his following.

> If you have no faith in their word,
> Ask the mountains,
> They will reveal the truth to you.

> Do you know who will also speak to you of God?
> It is the *chelil* of the horse Borak.
> The *chelil* which is strewn with buttons of gold,
> And from which hang splendid fringes.

> The *chelil* loves those men who fast,
> And those who spend their nights in
> Reading the books of God.

> It also loves the brave.
> The brave who strike with the saber
> And who cast into the dust
> The infidels and unbelievers.

Whoever owns it outstrips all others
Close to God, the Master of the world.
Whoever owns it should have a word
Which will never be gone back upon,
A saber always drawn
And a hand always open to the poor.

But that *chelil*,
I have never seen it on this earth.
I do not even know what color it is;
But I have been told of it
And I believe.

I do not know if I deceive myself as to the merit of these verses, but it seems to me that there are in that fragment a charm and a grandeur rarely offered by the works of the spirit among the most advanced nations. That last line, "But I have been told of it and I believe," would not detract from the most learned composition of a cultured literature. It expresses that which the faith of the believer holds of the most positive and most enthusiastic with a kind of skeptic grace. The officer whom I wanted to convince had the same impression. That start had put us both in a mood for poetry and I made a new appeal to the Chambi's memory.

Poets, among the Arabs, draw all their inspirations from the same sources. Religion, war, love, and horses, behold [that is] what they incessantly extol. Often the same song contains all these narrow and fertile elements of their whole life. God is asked to make victors of those who request it; horses are asked by those who own them to carry them to [their] Fatmas or Aychas. What a difference between that primitive and forceful poetry of the Arabs, so rich in its expatiations, but so grave in its themes, and our restless, tormented, capricious poetry which overturns all parts of heaven and earth to seek there the subjects of which it treats in its feverish and labored tongue!

The Chambi's memories were often gleaned with difficulty and most often we obtained only some snatches of songs which we would have liked to set down in their entirety. But verses are like diamonds which gleam with an even greater brilliance if they are not made into diadems or sprays.

Here, at random, follow some of the fragments which I tore from my odd visitor's memory. I believe that herein can be seen, as I see them, those immense shafts [of light] where limitless perspectives are disclosed.

> Turn your eyes towards the *douars* of Angad,
> Then lift them to the sky and count the stars;
> Think of the enemy where you have no friend,
> Think of our mountains, of their narrow paths.
> Come alone, she said to me, and be without a companion.

Either I am strangely misled by the charm which a life that will be forever dear to me has left in my memory, or there is in those lines that which the knowledge of nature contains of the greatest nobility and that which love holds of greatest passion. And what portrays more faithfully that chivalry to which Arab ways are still subject than this other stanza, also vividly come from the recollections of the Chambi:

> My courser becomes restive in front of my tent.
> He has seen the mistress of the rings ready to depart.
> It is today that we should die for the women of the tribe.

All those who have been present at combats in Africa know the role the women play in all the scenes of battle. It is for them that the gunpowder speaks. The response of all chieftains to overtures of peace made to them is: "*What would our women say if we did not fight? They would no longer want to prepare us couscous.*"

It is a great error to believe that Islam keeps the woman in a state of abjection from which only the miracles of the Christian faith could extricate her. The Moslem woman, on the contrary, has maintained among the men—whom her words launch into battle—that prestige which the queens of tournaments in the days of gallant deeds of warriors of the Middle Ages enjoyed.

The Chambi succeeded in reciting an entire song to us, in which the woman is simultaneously panegyrized with a profound sentiment of moral tenderness together with those outbursts of sensual passion, that wealth of ardent images which, since the *Song of Songs* (*The Song of Solomon*) in the Middle East, burst forth in all odes to love:

My sister[5] cannot be compared but with a trained mare
Who always brings up the rearguard
With a saddle sparkling with gold,
Ridden by a dashing horseman
Who knows how to lean forward
When the noise of gunpowder reverberates.

My sister is like a young she-camel
Returning from the Tell
In the midst of her companions,
Laden with precious cloths.

Her hair falls over her shoulders
And is as fine as silk.
It is like the black plumes of the male ostrich
When he watches over his young in the Sahara.

Her eyebrows, they are the *noûn*[6]
Which is found in the pages of the Koran;
Her teeth resemble polished ivory;
Her lips are stained with *kermès*;
Her breast, it is the snow that
Falls in the Djebel Amour.

O Time! Be accursed if she should come to forget me!
That would be like the gazelle which forgets its brother.

Only horses can dispute with women the privilege of an enthusiastic tenderness in the heart of a Moslem. The horse is, among the Arabs, raised to the dignity of a creature animated by intelligence. The horse Borak has his place in Paradise among the saints, houris, and prophets. We have seen what virtues his *chelil* has, that marvelous talisman which is the share of the true believer. Thus, all the suavity which the Arabs use to describe their women is used equally to depict the strong and fiery grace of their horses:

Sidi-Hamra owns a mare,
The gray of pebbles in a river,
Who does nothing but prance.

[5] Sister: the Arabs in their poetry so designate a mistress. See chapter 4, n. 13.
[6] *Noûn*: arc-shaped letter of the Arabic alphabet.

He owns a mare as red as
The blood which flows on holy days,[7]
Or like the heart of a rose.

He owns, moreover, a black mare
Like the male of the ostrich
Which wanders through deserted lands.

Lastly, he owns a dapple-gray mare
Who resembles the leopard
Given to our sultans as a gift.

Behold that which the Chambi declaimed to us in a voice just as caressing as if he had depicted for us the charms of the most marvelous beauties of the desert. He next said to us:

I desire a docile horse
That loves to champ the bit;
That is familiar with journeys;
That can endure hunger
And that can make in one day
The journey of five.
That it bear me to Fatma
That woman as powerful as
The Bey of Médéa
When he goes forth with
Goums and askars[8]
To the sound of flutes and drums.

The Arabs are as untiring in speech as they are in silence. They go to extremes in everything. They can be seen on horseback for days on end, devouring the plains, laughing at mountains; or they can be seen in front of their tents, lying on carpets, gaze fixed on the vast horizons, for an undetermined number of hours! My Chambi, had I not stopped him, would still be reciting desert poems to me. Gunpowder, horses, camels, the shrieks of young girls: that humble man had evoked all the sounds, all the colors, all the figures of his homeland. He was, in that respect, like a smoker of hashish, lost in that enchanted world.

---

[7] On holy days, among the Moslems, a large number of animals are bled and are then carved up and distributed to the poor.

[8] Askars: native infantry soldiers in the army of Morocco or any other Arabic-speaking country. [Translator's note]

But our life does not allow us to permit ourselves to be pervaded for long by poetry.[9] I put an end to a visit which had already taken up too much useful time. For the rest, I had extracted from it victorious arguments for my cause.

"I give in," said my interlocutor. "I agree with you that no peasant's memory will be ornamented in France or even, I believe, in any country in Europe, like that of the Chambi. Let us concede to the land of sun the facility of coloring all men's thoughts and language with the same hues as those of the sky."

"Let us thank God," I added, "for the gift of the realm of the imagination as a refuge to those who lead on a barren soil a life of misery and danger."

As for the Chambi, he scarcely troubled himself with the reflections he had just furnished us. He had resumed his resigned expression and placid attitude. As I asked him, upon bidding him farewell, what resources he counted on in his continual peregrinations, he opened his mouth and showed me, between his bronzed lips, those teeth of a dazzling whiteness which distinguish the sons of the desert: "He who has built the mill will not let it stand idle for lack of grist."

When he had gone I thought that that poor wretch carried, perhaps, beneath his rags, the two greatest treasures in this world: poetry and wisdom.

I would like to make known, in all their details, the customs of a country which today [1850] is forever linked to ours. I would like to do so for many reasons. Among us the greatest interest is aroused by that which appeals to the imagination. If it were possible to know all that the Arab spirit holds of verve, originality, and attraction, there would very swiftly be in France a truly unbounded admiration for Algeria. So, I also believe, would all European literatures benefit from the light shed on a people where climate, customs, and religion have united such a prodigious variety of poetic riches. James Fenimore Cooper[10] held in suspense the curiosity of an immense public with his

---

[9] General Daumas was then director of the Bureau of Algerian Affairs in the Ministry of War in France. [Translator's note]

[10] James Fenimore Cooper (1789–1851): American novelist born in the state of New York.

tales of American Indian tribes. The sons of the desert are men other than those of the American tribes. Among the peoples of Africa grace, intelligence, and the dazzlement of ancient civilizations blend with the forcefulness of the savage life. Those men who spend their time under the tent, who live by the spur and rifle, are familiar with the immortal poetry of the Koran and have on all things human a thousand insights full of subtlety. I shall endeavor to furnish proof of it.

Some people, I am assured, have become interested in that Chambi whom I recently brought on stage. I found myself lately in circumstances wholly similar to those in which I was at the time of the visit which I have recounted so precisely. I was discussing with the same officer that which is, I agree, an habitual preoccupation of my thoughts: an Arab land, its inhabitants, the studies of all kinds which it would furnish for curious and attentive natures in the vast region where, every year, moreover, our destinies become more intertwined. The Chambi suddenly presented himself to our view.

"I thought you had gone back to the desert again?" I said to him.

"Not at all," he replied. "I am staying here with some companions."

(I shall say, in passing, that there is at the moment here in Paris a group of Arabs, for the greater part from the Sahara, who have brought together in our midst their errant and blithe existences.)

"And what are you living on?"

He started to laugh with that intelligent and, if it may be expressed thus, convincing laughter of peoples who do not, like us, mislead with that play of expression.

"Listen," he said. "Every Sunday we go to a café. There someone says to us: smoke, drink coffee, and you will be paid. In effect, when we have smoked and drunk for several hours, someone gives us forty *douros*, and that is enough for us to live on all week."

At that point he laughed again and added a phrase whose picturesque irony is difficult to translate into our language, but which means almost the following: *The children of Mohammed profit from that which God has created expressly for feeding them: a nation of simpletons.*

Thus Gil Blas[11] and Guzmán de Alfarache[12] do not belong only to our regions. For behold, Africa also furnishes us with that type of man for whom the pavement of large cities is an inexhaustible field from which comes an infinity of crops. For a long time I had desired to gather the customary impressions which our country, our customs, our civilization cause travelers from Arab countries to experience. I resolved to profit from the Chambi's fresh visit to extract from an African mind a whole series of reasoned opinions on France. I began therefore an inquiry in which at first I asked my guest a few preliminary questions about Christians. See his first replies:

You do not pray, you do not fast, you do not perform your ablutions, you do not shave your heads, you are not circumcised, you do not bleed the animals which supply you with meat, you eat pork and drink fermented liquors which make you become similar to beasts; you have the infamy to wear a cap which does not bear [the image of] Sidna-Aïssa (Our Lord, Jesus Christ). Behold, that is what we have with which to reproach you. In exchange, we say: You fight well, your *aman* (pardon) is sacred, you do not demand tribute; you are polite, you are little given to lying, you love cleanliness. If, together with all that, you were able to say, just once, from the bottom of your heart: *"There is no other God but God and our Lord Mohammed is the envoy of God,"* no one would enter Paradise ahead of you.

More than one reader will certainly smile at certain passages of that tirade in which he will encounter ludicrous trivialities. Perhaps that reader should reflect before smiling. That singular reproach: "You have the infamy to wear a cap which does not bear [the image of] Our Lord, Jesus Christ," adheres precisely to that which gives to the Arab customs the greatest of grandeur and dignity. In that land of ancient traditions, nothing has changed. The sons hold it an honor to be clothed like their fathers. That ridiculous tyranny of fashion to which

11 Alain René Lesage (1668–1747): the author of *Gil Blas,* famous picaresque novel. [Translator's note]
12 Mateo Alemán (1547–1614?): Spanish novelist who owes his fame to one of the best of picaresque novels, *Guzmán de Alfarache.* [Translator's note]

the most sober spirits among us are obliged to submit is there [in the desert] something which is completely unknown. Garments, like customs, are under the protection of religion and draw from those august laws something of a particular gravity. What there is of absurdity in our accouterments has certainly been among the most powerful obstacles interposed between Arab ways and European influence.

Putting aside general considerations on the Christian race, I asked the Chambi what had appeared to him to be worthy of praise in France. Here is what I obtained from him:

There is in your land strict order. A man can travel day and night without disquiet. Your buildings are beautiful, your lighting admirable. Your carriages are comfortable; there is nothing in this world with which your steamships and your railroads can be compared. Among you are found foods and pleasures for all ages and all purses. You have an army organized by ranks, this one under that one. None of your cities lack infantry; your infantrymen are the ramparts of your country. Your cavalry is badly mounted, but marvelously equipped. The steel of your soldiers shines like silver. You have water and bridges in abundance. Your crops are well understood; you have one for each season. The eye does not cease to see your vegetables and fruits as your soil does not cease to produce them. We have found in your garden of baylic (the Jardin des Plantes) animals, plants, and trees of which our ancestors themselves had never heard mention. You possess that with which to satisfy the entire universe in silk, velours, precious stuffs, and gems. Lastly, what astounds us the most is the celerity with which you learn what is occurring at the most distant points.

Behold what is most assuredly a handsome eulogy of our civilization! It seems that we should exercise a great sway over a people who appreciate, in such a lively fashion, all the discoveries and all the resources of our minds; [but], unfortunately, the Arabs place in the judgments they make on themselves an intelligence just as keen as in the judgments they make on us. They are not savages, leading, through the sole impulse of necessity and habit, a life of which they do not understand the grandeur. What there is of profound charm, of strong attraction, in their free and perilous existence, they know better than we. Such can be judged by this vindication of Africa with which the Chambi caused his eulogy of our country to be followed:

Whereas your sky is incessantly cloudy, your sun of one or two days' [duration], no more, we have constant sun and a magnificent climate. If by chance the sky opens over us, an instant later it closes again, good weather reappears and warmth is restored to us. Whereas you are fixed to the earth by those houses you love and we detest, every two or three days we see a fresh land. In those migrations we have as an accompaniment war, the chase, young girls uttering shrieks of joy; herds of camels and sheep, which are God's blessing, wander along under our eyes; mares followed by their foals gambol around us.

You work like wretches; we do nothing. Our life is filled by prayer, war, love, the hospitality we give or receive. With respect to the hard labors of the soil, that is the work of slaves. Our herds, which are our fortune, live on God's domain. We have no need to till, cultivate, reap, or thresh. When we judge it necessary, we sell some camels or sheep or horses or wool. Then we buy the cereals which our existence requires and the most costly of those goods which the Christians take so much trouble to manufacture. Our women, when they love us, themselves saddle our horses, and when we set foot in the stirrup, they come to say to us, upon presenting us with our rifles: "O, my Lord! If it pleases God, you [shall] depart with fortune, you shall return with fortune."

Our land, in spring, in winter, in all seasons, resembles a carpet of flowers from which exudes the sweetest of scents. We have truffles and the *danoum* which is as good as the turnip; *drin* furnishes us with a precious food. We hunt the gazelle, the ostrich, the lynx, the hare, the rabbit, the leopard, the fox, the jackal, the *bekeur-el-ouhach* (antelope). *No one makes us pay taxes; no sultan rules us.*

Among you, hospitality is given in exchange for money. Among us, when one has said: "I am a guest of God," one will be answered: "Assuage your belly" and haste is made to wait on one.

If civilization received eulogies, at the same instant behold the desert, which is also well extolled. I would that that flow of words, translated with a scrupulous fidelity, would cause those people to ponder a little who are indignant that the Europeans and the native tribes have not already formed, in Algeria, one sole people, governed by the same laws.

Meditate upon each of these phrases and it will be seen that the task of our conquest is that of uniting the most opposite of elements. Whereas the presiding spirit of Europe is industry, the presiding spirit of the desert is idleness. Where the modern spirit pursues the, perhaps, chimeric idea of pacific domination, the spirit of ancient times is retained among the primitive peoples of Africa, who live inflamed by war. I do not despair, certainly, of the goal which our authority has set itself. But, to attain that goal, even with greater rapidity and surety, it is well not to conceal any of the obstacles which separate us from it.

It will be found that there are, perhaps, some very serious considerations there, apropos of the Chambi's conversation. The people who do not like to have on their minds the weight of serious thought will prefer to the preceding, no doubt, that which I yet have left to say.

I concluded from certain of his words that my visitor was a moralist and there is one subject with which moralists of all ages especially like to deal—that is women. I had nothing to regret about having started the Chambi on that topic. The philosopher of Ouargla put into his discourse—on the subject which will forever most occupy the madmen and the sages of all countries and all eras—a malicious verve, worthy of Rabelais[13] and Montaigne.[14] It was at first a series of dicta.

"Among you and among us," he said, "woman's guile is unequaled."

> They girdle themselves with vipers
> And they pin themselves with scorpions.
> The women's market is like that of falcons—
> He who goes there should be suspicious of them.
> They will make him forget his labors;
> They will destroy his renown;
> They will eat his fortune;
> They will give him a straw pallet for a shroud.

According to these dicta, which I could multiply, a species of

---

[13] François Rabelais (c. 1490–1553): French writer and physician.
[14] Michel Eyquem, Seigneur de Montaigne (1533–1592). French essayist.

rhymed proverbs—wherein good sense and poetry link themselves in a singular way—the Chambi gave us a complete tableau of customs which I desire to try to render. What it holds of profound originality will cause to be excused what might be, perhaps, somewhat offensive to certain ideas of our civilization and our country.

"Among us," said our Arab, "women like it that a man be always careful in his dress, fights well, has an ever open hand, rides a horse skillfully, and knows how to keep a secret. Behold what concerns the lover. With respect to the husband, it is necessary that he not forget for even one day the duties of marriage. Without that, his wife goes to find the *cadi* and from far away, when she first sees him, she starts shouting.

" 'O, my lord!' she says to him, 'there is no shame when one obeys one's religion. Well, then! I come in the name of my religion to accuse my husband. He is not a man, he does not look at me. Why should I stay with him?'

"The *cadi* answers her: 'O, my daughter! What are you complaining about? He feeds you well, he clothes you well, you have all you wish.' 'No, my lord,' she replies. 'I am neither fed nor clothed. If he does not accomplish that which is prescribed for him by our Lord Mohammed, I want a divorce.' The *cadi* then proclaims: 'You are right! The religion of women is love.'

"And almost always the divorce is decreed."

Many people go about saying that women are unfortunate in Moslem society. I did not pose that question to the Chambi, but if I had said: "Do you think that your women would wish to live under our law?" He would have answered me, I am sure: "They would regret the protective authority of the *cadi*."

I would prolong endlessly a topic, whose chief virtue should be brevity, should I desire to report everything that the inhabitant of the desert yet went on to picture for me concerning observations, maxims, poetry. Among the jumble of words and thoughts intermingled like capricious arabesques in that long interview, I noted one sentence in verse which I wish to quote at any price, for it bears the stamp of that pride, a distinctive trait of the Arab character, which cannot be disdained without danger by whomsoever is called upon to deal with Moslem peoples:

Remember that one ounce of honor
Is worth more than one *quintal* of gold.
Do not allow anyone to use you as a toy.
[In] the land where your pride suffers,
Quit it although its walls be built of rubies.

The author of *El Cid*[15] would have loved, I think, that poetry. Is it not stamped with a grandeur which recalls that pride which Castilian blood has drawn, without any doubt, from African veins? My Chambi was going to become for me an Abencérage[16] when I took leave of him upon giving him a *douro*. That Arab, who had already drawn some lessons from Paris, then revealed himself completely. He took the coin in his fingers and, raising it above his head, shouted: "See your father! Mine and that of all the world!"

I recount that which I have heard. With respect to the task of drawing conclusions, I leave it to those who love to disentangle the bizarre enigma of the human spirit.

[15] El Cid: in Spanish literature a title of Ruy, or Rodrigo, Díaz de Bivar, a champion of Christianity in the eleventh century. The Cid whose exploits were celebrated in the Castilian epic, *Poema de Mio Cid,* of unknown authorship, written about 1140, differs greatly from the historical figure but it is the Cid of the poem who became the ideal Spanish hero. [Translator's note]

[16] Abencerrajes or Abencérages: a fifteenth-century Moorish tribe which exercised great influence in the kingdom of Granada (Spain). Its rivalry with the Zegríes was one of the causes of the downfall of the kingdom of Granada. Ginés Pérez de Hita composed in the sixteenth century a *History of the Zegríes and the Abencerrajes* from which Chateaubriand drew inspiration. [Translator's note]

GLOSSARY

Aâchera: she-camel which has just given birth

Aâcheub: generic term for plants

Aâdet esserdj: custom of the saddle

Aâgueub: camel-sinew thread

Aâkeud echikh: knot of the sheik

Aàkuif: plant

Aâmayre: nose bag

Aârare: resinous tree

Aarirb: plant

Aâsaba: narrow cords

Aâssa: flock of sheep

Aasseur: daytime (or afternoon)

Aâtatouche: camel chair

Aâzara: servants

Âdeme: plant

Ademi: largest species of gazelle

Adjaïze: old women

Adjerem: plant, shrub

Âdjouza: go-betweens, intermediaries

Aeuchet el zemel: special tent

Afli: plant

Aga, or *Agha*: title of respect

Agad: falcon's prey

Aguereub: scorpion

Ahna ou ben el mera: "I and the son of woman"

Akeud: bond, pact

Alfa: esparto grass

Alned: shrub

Aman: pardon

An cha Allah: God willing

Aokha: sheepskins

Aoudad: *see* Lerouy

Arfedj: shrub

Ataïah!: a cry

Azbiân: plant

Azir: plant

Bageul: plant

Bahara: species of falcon

Bakia: wooden drinking cup

Baylic: botanical garden

Beajiq: plant

Bedoui: nomad, desert dweller

Bekeur-el-ouhach: antelope

Bekra: mature she-camel

Belbal: shrub

Belghra: Moroccan slippers

Ben deraou: son of his weapon

Benica: head covering

Ben-naamàn: plant

Berana: species of falcon

Berrani: foreigner, stranger

Bessem Allah, Allah ou kebeur: In

the Name of God, God is the
mightiest
Bethom: shrub
Bezima: buckles
Bezimat el gueursi: brooches
Biaz: falconer
Bibache: plant
Bine: plant
Boualal: rats
Bou chelalle: camel disease
Boudjou: Algerian coin
Bou-kharis: plant
Bou-nagar: plant
Burnoose: Arab cloak

Cadi: judge
Cedria: waistcoat
Chabir: spurs
Chachia: woolen cap
Chaouch(s): policeman, policemen
Chegaâ: plant
Cheggag: cracks in the soles of the
feet
Chehada: last sacrament
Chelil: silk housing on horse's
croup
Chemâl: net used on she-camels
Chenine: sour milk; *see also leben*
Chérifs: descendants of the Prophet
Cherrima: saw
Cheurfaa: upper class
Chibouta: goatskin
Chiehh: artemisia (*Herba alba*)
Chikh: sheik(s)
Chouaf, chouafin: scout, scouts
Couscous: Arab dish

Danoum: vegetable
Debabe: large flies

Deglet en nour: "luminous" date,
of transparent appearance
Deguig: wheat flour
Deheun: rancid butter
Délim: male ostrich
Delou: water bucket
Dereuf: shrub
Derine: plant
Deroua: camel's hump
Deubàl: plant
Difa: hospitality
Dif rebi: guest sent by God
Dil-el-fàr: plant
Djad: shrub
Djamous: horn
Djebel: a mountain
Djebira: saddlebag
Djedâa: three-year-old camel
Djedi: fawns
Djefen: shrub
Djelàb: shrub
Djeld sebaa ala dohor el beugra:
lion's skin on a cow's frame
Djeliba: flock of ostriches
Djellale: horse blankets
Djelliba: herd of gazelles
Djeloud: honey sacks
Djemâa: assembly of elders
Djemel: camel
Djemir: plant
Djereub: scab
Djieud: military nobleman
Djouad: military noblemen
Dolly: species of leopard
Douars: tents pitched in
circles
Doulamas: doctors of law
Douro(s): coin(s)
Drâa: plant

Drin: plant (*Arthraterum pungens*)

Dya: blood money

Ech-chabrag: shrub

Ech-cheliath: plant

Ech-cherirah: plant

Ed-delnef: plant

Ed-demrâne: plant

Ed-djedar: shrub

Ed-doum: shrub

En-nagad: shrub

En-nedjem: plant

En-neguig: plant

En-netil: plant

Er-ràbi: plant

Er-reguigue: plant

Er-reguir: shrub

Er-reteum: shrub

Er-reumt: plant

Eslem: verb form, to save

Es-sad: shrub

Es-salian: shrub

Es-sambari: plant

Es-sedra: shrub (mastic)

Es-sefar: shrub

Es-seleuse: plant

Es-senagh: plant

Es-sigue: plant

Et-tafegh: shrub

Et tàlem: plant

Ettharf: shrub

Ez-zafzàf: plant

Ez-zagza: plant

Ez-zit: shrub

Faâl: camel destined for stud

Faâla: sire camel

Faâl ihydje: camel's bugle

Fal chine: bad omen

Fantasia: show; often a display of horsemanship and prowess with weapons

Fass: mattocks

Fatahh: religious invocation

Fedjeur: daybreak

Feldja: tent material

Felidje: tent material

Ferou: shrub

Ferouga: barren she-camel

Ferrache: beds (carpets)

Fertass: bald

Fessy: caps

Fil: shrub

Filaly: morocco leather

Gaad: lookout

Gachouche: lure

Garah: three-year-old ostrich

Garthoufa: plant

Ghàres: shrub

Ghebir: plant

Ghedda: camel disease

Ghedir: ponds

Gherara: sack

Ghoche: sheep disease

Ghrelem: flock of four hundred sheep

Ghrezal: gazelle

Ghrezala: doe of the gazelle

Goôud: mature camel

Goulada: horse collar

Goum: troop of horsemen armed for war

Guedra: copper cooking pot for meat

Guefass: gauntlet

Guehouân: plant

Guelgelàne: plant

Guelmouna: hood of the burnoose
Guerade: fleas
Guerbas: goatskins
Guergue: boots
Guessaa: wooden vessels
Gueteum: shrub
Guethof: shrub (*Atriplex halimus*)
Guetifa: bed
Guezahh: shrub
Guiz: plant

Habara: guinea fowl
Habaya: woolen chemise or shirt
Hachy: three-year-old camels
Hadak houa: that one there, that is he
Hader: townsman
Hadj: sandy colocynth (*Citrullus colocynthis*)
Ha houa: there it is
Haïk: woolen outer garment
Hakem: magistrate
Hama: game animal or fowl
Hamal: sacks
Hamale el aâtatouche: litter curtains
Hamimeuch: plant
Hamma: plant
Hammaze: thief
Hamous: charge
Ha ou: there it is
Haouadjej: camel litters
Haouar: suckling camel
Haouly: head covering
Haouya: camel pack-saddles
Haref: plant
Harmel: plant
(*El*) *Hayi rah hena*: there is someone about

Hazame: woolen belts
Heug: four-year-old camel
Heulm: plant
Hhar: plant
Houache: bison or wild ox
Houbara: bustard
Houris: nymphs in Mohammedan Paradise

Ida djat el aïn fel aïn Tekoun chetara fel idain: should eye meet eye, celerity shows itself in the wrists
Igthàn: shrub
Ihydje: camel call
Islam: resignation

Kadouma: small hatchet
Karneb: plant
Karteum: shrub
Kate: complete suit of clothing
Kelokh: shrub
Kerat: plant
Kerbouss: pommel
Kerkaz: plant
Kermès: antimony
Keubda: liver
Keumbid: falcon's hood
Khaufeur: plant
Khebir: plant
(*El*) *kheïl lel bela, el begeur lel fekeur, el ybeul lel khela*: horses for combat, oxen for poverty, camels for the desert
Khelala: silver clasp
Khelfa: replacement
Khemoun: plant
Kher-eurby: God's blessing
Kher-ouby: curved-horned sheep

Kheud: plant
Khodar: shrub
Khorchef: shrub
Khrabya: clay jar
Khralfa mtâa redjal: men's sleep-
ing chamber
Khreima: furnished tent
Khreléa: dried meat
Khremass: watchman
Khriana: robbery
Khrodmi cheurr: knife of evil
Khrolkhral: ankle bracelets
Khrolkhrale: anklets
Khrotefa: rapine
Koheul: sulphur of antimony
Koubar: shrub
Koubba: holy man's tomb
Kratem: rings
Ksar, Kuesour: village
Ksibeur: plant
Kueca: woman's garment
Kuerabiche: cushions
Kuerboube: four-horned sheep
Kuerkuera: sternum (breastbone)
Kuerraba: lockets
Kuertem: shrub
Kuesob: plant
Kuesour: *see Ksar*
Kuettane el malty: cotton cloth
Kuikoute: plant

Larth: shrub
Layahh: distracter, distraction
Lazal: shrub
Leben: sour milk (*Chenine*)
Ledena: plant
Ledjerass: tiny jingle-bells
Lefâ: carpet viper
Legha: newly calved she-camel

Lella: plant
Lerouy (Aoudad): Barbary sheep
Lezoul: plant

Mâarouf: alms
Maha: wild white doe
Maharema: morocco leather belts
Mahari(s): racing camel(s)
Mahazema: cartridge clip
Mâk: plant
Mana: countersign
*Mayâreff chi lel Behaire, et-tob-
Ghèr elli rebah*: No one knows
the medicine of camels but he
who has bred some
Mecherahhin: provocateurs
Mechith: plant
Meddah: bards
Medjil: plant
Medol: straw hat
Meguil: a halt en route
Mekadem, Mekadinn: arbitrator(s)
Meker: shrub
Mekhranga: cloves
Mekhreloul: weanling camel
Mekhrengua: necklaces
Mektaa: lengths of cloth
Melahh: plant
Melebda: hunter's blind
Melyaca: bracelets
*(El) mera bela hazame, ou el aouda
bela ledjame*: the woman with-
out her girdle and the mare with-
out her bridle
Meradjen: handled copper cups
Merakh: shrub
Merkeb: desert hillocks shaped like
ships

Meroueud: sliver of polished wood

Mesaoudin: horse marking indicating good luck

(*el*) *Metmir rahala*: ambulatory storehouses

Metnân: plant

Metreud: wooden platter

Meudjeza: sickle for sheep-shearing

Mezerague: share, portion

Mezoueud: ration sacks

Mezrag: lance

Mordjem: cooking pot

Mourar: plant

Mrar: plant

Mtâ rebi ia el moumenin: that which belongs to God or believers

Mysseur: she-camel in season

Naga: she-camel

Naga kuessab kher min fareus saadi: a fertile she-camel is worth more than a joyous horseman

Nasi: shrub

Nebala: species of falcon

Nechâa: bad omen

Neda: dew

Neddabat: mourners

Nedjeuss: camel disease

Nehheb el id chedida, ou souag el baâida, ou dar djedida: I want a closed hand, distant markets (and) a new house each day

Nezaf: lazy baggage camel

Nhar refoude: the "carrying-off" of a bride

Nif: amour propre, self-respect

Noûn: letter of Arabic alphabet

Nous el leïl: midnight

Ouadâa: fête or feast

Oubeur: camel hair

Ouchâm: plant

Oudene-en-nadja: plant

Oueera: bush

Oughrlila: vest

Oukerif-el-ouhach: antelope fawn

Ould aâchar: suckling camel

Ould el boun: two-year-old camel

Ouled bou gleubtin: two-year-old ostrich

Ouled gleub: ostrich between one and two years old

Ounaiss: earrings

Ous aâda: pillows

Ousaïdes: pillows

Ousiga: reprisals

Oussera: shrub

Ouye: call to a falcon

Ra hena: he is there

Rahil: nomadic migration

Ral: one-year-old ostrich

Rana akeud: pact, bond

Razzia(s): foray(s)

Rebâa: five-year-old camel

Reguime: plant

Rekass: swift couriers

Rekiza: tent poles

Reumda: female ostrich

Rinne: species of gazelle

Robaï: molars

Rouina: grilled flour

Sag-el-gherabe: plant

Salat el djenaza: prayer for the dead

Salat el mokteâat: burial chant
Sebkha: salt flat or pan
Seboula: dagger
Sekakri: merchant
Selem: to deliver (save); *see Eslem*
Semaid: jesses
Semmâte: saddlebag
Sensela: chains
Seroual: trousers
Seroun: game animal or fowl
Sine: species of gazelle
Slougui: saluki
Slouguia: saluki bitch
Slouguïa: place name
Slougui men bad haouli, ou radjel men bad soumeïn: the saluki after two years and the man after two fasts, if they are not worth anything, there is no hope.
Soff: federation, political alliance
Sor: plant
Souar: pairs of bracelets
Sourate: chapters of the Koran
Stara: saddle cover

Taga: resinous plant
Tags: rugs to divide a tent
Tague hambeul: carpet
Tahan: cuckold
Tahh: he is fallen
Taka: litter peepholes
Takht: camel coach; *Takhts er-Rúm* (pl.)
Tandjera: copper cooking pot
Tarahh: morocco leather skins
Tassa: copper drinking vessels
Techaha: training of the horse for the chase

Techouf, choufel el hama, ou temchy, mechit el haytama: she sees like the owl and travels like the tortoise
Tedjenâa: protection against flies
Téhan: camel disease
Téhha: falling upon
Tellis: camel load
Temag: boots
Temagues: woman's boots
Terakel: species of falcon
Terbigue: theft
Tergou: ghosts of those who have died violent deaths
Teskir: shrub
Thaïr el horr: pedigreed bird
Thaïr el horr ala haseul ma iqtrebochi: a pedigreed bird, when captured, does not become downcast
Thaleb: tutor
Ticheret: plant
Tiguentcuse: shrub
Tis-el-djebel: mountain goat
Tolba: scribe
Trabag: leggings

Wehrgeld: blood money (German)

Yanthite: shrub
Yatagan: knife, or saber
Yathithar: shrub
Ybal: troop of 100 she-camels
Ybeul: troop of camels
Ydjefeur: camel's rut

Zaouïa(s): religious establishment(s)

Zateur: shrub
Zebeud: civet musk
Zebeun: horseman's share of the booty
Zebeur: allies' reward
Zeboudje: shrub

Zedja: fleece
Zemmal: hunt servant
Zerga: the blue, meaning the sea
Zouzál: gelded camel
Zyara: visit

SELECTED BIBLIOGRAPHY

Daumas, Melchior Joseph Eugène. *The Horses of the Sahara*. Translated by Sheila M. Ohlendorf. Austin: University of Texas Press, 1968.

Doughty, Charles M. *Travels in Arabia Deserta*. New and Definitive Edition. 2 vols. London: Jonathan Cape, 1936.

Furlonge, Geoffrey. *The Lands of Barbary*. London: John Murray, 1966.

Gardner, Brian. *The Quest for Timbuctoo*. London: Cassell & Co., 1968.

Jarrett, H. R. *Africa*. London: Macdonald & Evans, 1962.

Ogrizek, Doré, ed. *North Africa*. New York: McGraw-Hill Publishing Co., 1955.

Reclus, Élisée. *Africa*. Vol. 2. *The Earth and Its Inhabitants*. Edited by A. H. Keane. New York: D. Appleton and Co., 1893.

Tweedie, Maj. Gen. W. *The Arabian Horse: His Country and People*. Edinburgh: Blackwood & Sons, 1894.

Vogel, Zdeněk. *Reptile Life*. Translated by Margot Schierl. London: Spring Books, c. 1950.

Wentworth, Lady. *The Authentic Arabian Horse*. London: George Allen & Unwin, 1943.

Wentworth, Lady. *Thoroughbred Racing Stock*. London: George Allen & Unwin, 1938.

INDEX

DATE DUE